Praise for
Winning at Home

"It's no secret that we are in a battle for the family—our families—the haven that is essential to healthy and thriving human beings. Winning the battle of course starts at home with healthy, attuned, godly parents who are courageous, loving, and kind. Parents who are present and have hard, important conversations focused on bringing help and light to the darkness and challenges of this life. In *Winning at Home*, Dan always communicates a practical biblical truth that is applicable to daily life. I think you will find some amazing insights that are relevant for our times and will speak life into your family..."

— **Dr. Tim Clinton**, president of the American Association of Christian Counselors, co-host of *Family Talk* with Dr. James Dobson, and executive director of Liberty University Global Center for Mental Health, Addiction, and Recovery

"Dan and his team have written an outstanding book for all of us searching how to 'win at home.' This book covers some crucial, hard topics in a solid biblical way that is easily digestible. Dan is an incredible teacher whom I have spent time with, and I have seen first-hand the results of his efforts. *Winning at Home* is a must-read. Thank you guys for putting all this down on paper for us to learn from."

— **Willie Robertson**, CEO of Duck Commander

Winning at Home

WINNING
at HOME

Tackling the Topics that
Confuse Kids and Scare Parents

DAN SEABORN

SALEM
BOOKS
an imprint of Regnery Publishing
Washington, D.C.

Unless otherwise marked, all scriptures are taken from the Holy Bible, New International Version®, NIV®. Copyright © 1973, 1978, 1984, 2011 by Biblica, Inc. ® Used by permission of Zondervan. All rights reserved worldwide. www.zondervan.com. The "NIV" and "New International Version" are trademarks registered in the United States Patent and Trademark Office by Biblica, Inc.®

Scripture quotations marked AMP are taken from the Amplified® Bible, Copyright © 1954, 1958, 1962, 1964, 1965, 1987 by The Lockman Foundation. Used by permission. www.lockman.org

Scriptures marked ESV are taken from ESV® Bible (The Holy Bible, English Standard Version®), copyright © 2001 by Crossway, a publishing ministry of Good News Publishers. Used by permission. All rights reserved.

Scriptures marked KJV are taken from the King James Version, public domain.

Scriptures marked NLT are taken from the Holy Bible, New Living Translation. Copyright © 1996, 2004, 2015 by Tyndale House Foundation. Used by permission of Tyndale House Ministries, Carol Stream, Illinois 60188. All rights reserved.

Scripture quotations marked NRSV are taken from the New Revised Standard Version of the Bible. Copyright © 1946, 1952, and 1971 National Council of the Churches of Christ in the United States of America. Used by permission. All rights reserved.

Salem Books™ is a trademark of Salem Communications Holding Corporation.

Regnery® is a registered trademark and its colophon is a trademark of Salem Communications Holding Corporation.

Cataloging-in-Publication data on file with the Library of Congress

ISBN: 978-1-68451-307-9
eISBN: 978-1-68451-322-2

Library of Congress Control Number: 2022941044

Published in the United States by
Salem Books
An Imprint of Regnery Publishing
A Division of Salem Media Group
Washington, D.C.
www.SalemBooks.com

Manufactured in the United States of America

10 9 8 7 6 5 4 3 2 1

Books are available in quantity for promotional or premium use. For information on discounts and terms, please visit our website: www.SalemBooks.com.

This book is dedicated to my family. I grew up in an imperfect family, and I'm a husband, dad, and papa in an imperfect family now. Out of that, we're working to learn and grow from our mistakes and also to celebrate our victories. I pray God uses this book to make a difference for other families that are imperfect, just like ours!

CONTENTS

Introduction   xi

CHAPTER 1
Parenting from True Identity   1

CHAPTER 2
Parenting a Child with Mental Health Concerns   19

CHAPTER 3
Handling Technology Well   39

CHAPTER 4
Parenting in a Hypersexualized World   57

CHAPTER 5
Gender and Sexuality   77

CHAPTER 6
Developing an Appreciation for Scripture   103

CHAPTER 7
It Takes a Team   119

CHAPTER 8
Helping Parents Promote and Model Good Interpersonal
Skills and Boundaries   135

CHAPTER 9
I'm Your Parent First and Friend Second   155

CHAPTER 10
I Love You No Matter What   171

CHAPTER 11
Parenting Adult Children   189

Conclusion   209
About the Contributors   211
Recommended Resources   215

INTRODUCTION

My wife Jane and I have been married for nearly forty years, and we have four kids and seven grandkids. As you can imagine, we've learned a lot along the way! Some of what we've learned came from trying out new things that succeeded. But other lessons came from our missteps and well-intentioned, but wrong, choices. I hope you'll be able to gain some wisdom from our highs and lows without having to make the same mistakes we did!

My life in ministry started with me serving as a youth pastor and then a family life pastor for about a decade. After working full-time in a church during that period, I felt God leading me to start Winning At Home in 1995, and I have been leading the ministry since then. What started out as me traveling and speaking at churches, companies, and nonprofit organizations has now grown into a multisite ministry that offers speakers, counselors, and coaches to people at all ages and stages of family development and also produces resources and events geared toward helping them lead Christ-centered homes.

In this book, I will partner with several of the credentialed counselors, coaches, and pastors who work with me here at the ministry; they will each contribute to chapters that focus on their specific areas of training and experience. Together, we'll address many of the challenging topics that you're facing as you navigate raising children and teens in a world that doesn't always share our values.

This book will address some complex issues that you may not hear addressed in faith-based settings very often. We hope and pray that this will help parents with kids of all ages to handle challenging situations in ways that honor God.

Dan Seaborn

PARENTING FROM TRUE IDENTITY

Dan Seaborn

We're starting with identity in Chapter 1 because this lies at the core of how we parent. The following chapters will all focus heavily on your children, but this chapter will primarily focus on you—because if we aren't intentional about being aware of our own values and priorities, we very likely will unintentionally pass some things along to our kids that we don't want them to inherit. In other words, if we don't understand ourselves as fully as possible, we will probably project our insecurities, triggers, frustrations, and unmet expectations of ourselves onto our kids. None of us mean to do this, and none of us want to do it. But that's the tricky thing about values and priorities. We will pass them on, because we will naturally punish or celebrate our kids disproportionally in the areas where we have strong opinions.

Think about the parent who is a little *too* into their child's sports team. Or the parent who pushes pageants or certain professions onto their kids. If we as parents aren't okay with ourselves and don't know where our value comes from, we can fall into a pattern of trying to live vicariously through our children, hoping they will accomplish some of the things that we failed to accomplish when we were younger. On the face of it, that might not seem like a bad thing. But all you have to do is go online and search for "sports dad" or "stage mother" to find stories and experiences of people who got too carried away and tried to achieve some of the things they hadn't in their own lives through their children. That's not to say that if you don't figure out your own identity, you'll definitely find yourself going that far. But if you aren't reasonably secure in your own identity, then you are likely to project some of your hopes and dreams onto your children in unhealthy ways.

This part of the discussion is a nuanced one though, because it's absolutely possible to encourage your kids to do their best and to excel in sports or school or work without it coming from an unhealthy place in your own heart. In fact, encouraging them to excel at those activities is a good thing. That's what makes this so hard. You have to do the interior work yourself to figure out what your motivations are and where you might be encouraging your kids in a certain direction not because it's best for them, but in an attempt to make up for your own feelings of inadequacy or lack of success. This can show up in encouraging them to date a lot, to be fashionable, to drive the "right" car, or any number of things. But this chapter will be less about the specific ways this can play out negatively for your kids and more about how to find security and stability in your own identity.

It Starts with You

Much of our culture is driven by status or achievement. You may know this by the phrase "keeping up with the Joneses," or the more recent idea of conspicuous consumption—buying things that are expensive mostly due to the fact that they're expensive. Of course, some people just really like rare sneakers or expensive watches or fancy cars or designer handbags, but a good chunk of the people who are using those things are (at least partly) doing so because they are status symbols. It's a simple way to alert anybody else who is "in the know" that you know about a specific item, and that you have the ability to pay for it.

Or maybe your experience with an achievement-driven approach to life is that you've spoken to people who already make enough money to live comfortably and they're talking about wanting a promotion. When you ask why, they don't really have a reason other than because it's the next rung on the ladder. If we don't check those attitudes in ourselves, we will be approaching life, and parenting, with the underlying belief that getting to that next level or buying that next expensive thing will bring us some kind of satisfaction. We don't really say those things out loud, and I think that's partly because we know how silly it would sound. We know that every previous achievement or purchase was exciting for a short time, but then the newness wore off. New promotions come with new headaches. New cars get dirty or scratched. Expensive clothes require special care to the point that it's a little risky to actually wear them outside the house. New homes lose their luster—even if you build a brand-new one!

It isn't my goal to discourage anybody; I actually think what I'm sharing here is encouraging if you're willing to change your perspective. Because if you've been chasing achievement or status, you may have been surprised to find that it's not fulfilling you in the way you hoped it would. And for some reason, when we do something that doesn't work, our first reaction is to think that doing more of the thing that didn't work might be the solution! I'm not trying to pick on anybody reading this right now, because I see that behavior in my own life, too. In fact, I'll share more specifics in a bit. But the truth is that material things *can't* satisfy us. And success can't, either.

The sooner we realize that chasing things and success will ultimately leave us unfulfilled, the sooner we can move on to pursuing our true identity—who we are called to be in Christ. You may be tempted to write this off because you know I'm a pastor, so this is what I'm "supposed" to talk about. But I'm not sharing this out of a sense of obligation; I'm sharing this because

I've seen it play out countless times. Since Winning At Home is a nonprofit organization, part of my responsibility is to raise money to keep it funded. That means I'm talking to very wealthy and very successful people on a pretty regular basis. I've spoken to people who have more money than I could make in ten lifetimes who are stressed out about money. I can't personally put myself in their shoes and understand why they feel that way, but they tell me that when you lose money in the stock market or you have to pay for a big, unexpected expense, you feel the pinch no matter how much money you have. Like I said, I don't get it, but I really have had these conversations with people who have so much money that 10 percent of it would solve all my money-related concerns for the rest of my life.

But I want to make it clear that I'm not immune to this. I still catch myself thinking that my value lies in how well my last speaking event went. Or in how the ministry I founded is running. Or how my kids and grandkids are doing in life. But I want to share what I do that gets me reoriented when I get off track from finding my identity in Christ.

My Practice of Listening to God

What I'm going to share here is a habit that I've been practicing for more than twenty-five years. I've kept at it for so long because God has used my "listening time" to comfort me, challenge me, mold me, and guide me. I'm intentionally describing it with some words that highlight the positive emotions involved in the process and others that highlight the negative emotions involved. That's on purpose. The process of growth and surrender is a process of letting go and giving up. And those are not comfortable things. But they lead to growth and to places where God keeps working on me.

As I describe my process, just know that this is not the only way to practice something like this. Many people do something similar by going for a walk out in nature. Others practice some form of meditation. Others are more like Brother Lawrence, whose conversations and letters were turned into the Christian classic *The Practice of the Presence of God* and described how he would do his cooking and cleaning in the kitchen at a monastery while putting all of his attention on God. I mention all of those things before I describe my own practice because I don't want anybody to think mine is the only way, or the best way. Whatever practice helps you get quiet before God and connect with Him is the version that will be best for you.

Having said all that, here's what I do. I go to a quiet place in my home (that might not exist in your home if your kids are young!), or I close the door to my office at work and spend some time in the silence intentionally listening for God. I like to have a pen and paper with me because that helps me to get any thoughts out of my head and written somewhere so I don't have to work hard to remember them; I find that if I keep trying to remind myself to do things like *Make that phone call*, then I can't really spend time listening for God. I'll get so focused on working to keep track of the to-do list in my mind that I will lose focus on Him.

I learned this practice from a woman named Mary Geegh. When I met Mary, she was ninety years old and living in a nursing home near the church where I was a youth pastor. She had been a missionary in India and had written about her experiences in a book called *God Guides*.[1] As I read it, I was shocked at the stories about her faith and God's faithfulness. I was so shocked that I asked her if the stories in the book were actually true. She told me that they were and offered to teach me how to listen to God.

I should clarify that during my listening time, I don't "hear" God audibly. This time when I quiet myself is not about a conversation in the usual sense that we think of. But God brings thoughts to my mind; He encourages me and prompts me to grow during these times. When I was learning this practice from Mary, I remember going back to her with some questions after a few weeks. At one point, I wanted her guidance on a specific leading I was sensing. I told her, "I think God is telling me to go and ask for forgiveness. But it's from somebody that I haven't talked to in a long time. I actually don't even think they'll remember me." Mary smiled as she looked at me and said, "Oh yes, that sounds right." That didn't make much sense to me at the time, but today I definitely understand what she was talking about.

---

[1] You can find Mary's book for sale on Amazon or at winningathome.com.

God has used my listening time to encourage me and help me to grow in a huge number of ways that have required surrender and a "dying to self" that I never could have imagined. If you're reading this and thinking, *Well, that doesn't sound appealing!* I understand where you're coming from. It's not a pleasant process. But I've found that God is inviting me into those moments because He knows what is best and healthiest for me. And He knows that, left to my own devices, I will inevitably value the wrong thing. Thomas Merton writes beautifully about what it looks like for us to value the wrong thing:

> All sin starts from the assumption that my false self, the self that exists only in my own egocentric desires, is the fundamental reality of life to which everything else in the universe is ordered. Thus, I use up my life in the desire for pleasures and the thirst for experiences, for power, honor, knowledge and love, to clothe this false self and construct its nothingness into something objectively real. And I wind experiences around myself and cover myself with pleasures and glory like bandages in order to make myself perceptible to myself and to the world, as if I were an invisible body that could only become visible when something visible covered its surface.[2]

---

[2] Thomas Merton, *New Seeds of Contemplation* (Norfolk, VA: New Directions Books, 1961), 34–35.

It may be helpful to go back and read through that quote again—but more slowly this time, because it's astoundingly powerful. It's a big, dense idea that he's getting at here. What Merton does in this passage is lay out exactly what God works to remove from us when we fully listen and fully surrender to Him. When we spend time listening to God, He will call us to let go of things that we've "covered" ourselves with, to use Merton's language. So don't be surprised if God uses your listening time to show you some areas of your life that He invites you to change. You'll see some of your habits and attitudes and relationships in a new light—and that will be very intimidating at first.

In fact, our kneejerk reaction will be to hold onto and protect these things at all costs! Because we think that what we're being asked to let go of is actually *us*. We think that if we forgive, we won't be strong anymore. That if we admit to being wrong, we won't be wise anymore. That if we admit wrongdoing, we won't be respected anymore. But what God knows (and what we learn if we're obedient when He leads us) is that there isn't actually a connection between any of those things in the first place. You don't become less strong by forgiving. You don't become less wise by admitting you got something wrong. You don't become less respected by admitting fault.

Instead, we come to learn that our true identity is who we are in Christ, and that can't be impacted by anything anybody else says, does, or thinks. This is almost impossible to believe until you go through the process of letting go and "dying to self." Because most of our interactions with other people are situations where if one person wins, that probably means the other person loses. The amazing thing is that with God, it's not like that. He's not trying to get us to let go of things so He can gain something at our expense. He's inviting us to let go of things because He knows what's best for us—and because He *wants* what's best for us! I like to remind myself that He always has my best interests in mind. Often, it doesn't look that way to me, but He does. Just as we make our family rules because we're trying to protect our kids and set them up for success, so does God.

Things to Avoid
Don't get caught up in the ups and downs.

If you're finding your identity in any of the temporary and changeable things happening around you, you will most likely find yourself feeling great when things are smooth, and terrible when they aren't. If you tie your identity to things that *cannot* satisfy, you're completely at the mercy of your circumstances. That means when things at work are going well, you'll be a more engaged and positive parent. But when they aren't, you may be more detached or negative. Or when your kids are succeeding at school or in their extracurricular pursuits, then you're riding high. But if they're struggling in a class or don't make the team, you're feeling down and discouraged. In other words, when your identity is attached to changeable circumstances, you become less predictable and reliable for your kids. That's part of the reason that finding your identity in Christ is so important:

because life will be full of constantly changing circumstances. No matter how healthy or rich or successful you are, you can't insulate yourself from tough circumstances.

Don't make your kids' pursuits about you.

You can tell you're finding your identity in what your kids do when you're more disappointed than they are that they didn't get picked to be on a certain sports team. Or when they're excited to tell you that they were runner-up in some contest and your first thought is about how second place isn't the goal. These are not hypothetical examples. We probably all know parents who think like this. We might *be* parents who think like this. And when we're finding our identity in our kids' performances, then it's a big blow when they lose a basketball game or get eliminated from a spelling bee or have an experiment go haywire at a science fair. And that's just addressing things that happen in lower-stakes arenas of life; never mind how we would feel if they flunked out of college or stopped going to church or started dating somebody we don't approve of. Or if they were making even more destructive life choices than that.

This isn't to say that we won't be affected by what happens with our kids. We will still be disappointed when things don't go well, and we can absolutely still talk to our kids about any of these things. But when we are coming from a healthier place within ourselves, we'll be able to keep those disappointments and failures in proper perspective. And our approach will be about what is best for our kids, not what would make us feel less like we made mistakes as their parents.

Don't just tell them what you would do.

We'll all be tempted to give our kids advice based on how we would handle a situation they're facing if it were happening to us at our current stage of life. But that's actually not very helpful because they're *not* at our stage of life. In other words, we've probably learned not to let immature comments from people we aren't close to impact us very much, but giving that advice to our kids won't help them with where they find themselves today. It's important that we put ourselves in their shoes as much as possible, and that requires realizing that the way we naturally want to handle things isn't the perfect (or only) way to do it.

Don't let your hurts cloud your judgment.

It's very easy to be triggered into memories of our own teenaged selves when we see our kids do a certain thing or start thinking a certain way. We start to think we can predict exactly what comes next for them because we remember what came next for us. So if concerts were where we ran into drugs or bad influences, we assume that's why they want to go to live music events. Or if we had kids when we were seventeen or eighteen, we want to stop them from ever having crushes or dating anybody until they're old enough to care for a child of their own. But if we're thinking in those terms, we're likely to do a good amount of harm in the name of "protecting" our children. As I got into my adult years, I realized this was what motivated my dad to put many overly restrictive rules in place in our home while I was growing up. For instance, I wasn't allowed to go to my school's sporting events. I found out later it was because when he was younger, my dad and his friends had gone under the bleachers and gotten themselves into trouble with their actions. Your rules may be a little less "on the nose" than that one, but it will still be helpful for you to examine whether you're making some rules based on *your* behavior in the past rather than on your child's personality or behavior in the present.

Don't try to mold them to your personality.

When you're parenting from your true identity, you don't feel the need to mold your children to be just miniature versions of you. Instead, you can see them for the uniquely gifted and uniquely flawed individuals that they are—and instead of trying to make them better versions of yourself, you will desire to empower them to be themselves. Having that support from you and the knowledge that you are cheering for them to develop their own personality, likes, and dislikes will actually free them up to be themselves.

You've probably heard people talk about their achievements as being driven by a desire to win their parents' love or approval. And some parents might even withhold those things in an attempt to push their kids to achieve more and more. If you're tempted to do that, I hope you'll ponder this question Paul David Tripp asks in his book *Parenting*: "Could it be that your desire

for success has caused you to exercise a level of control that actually is in the way of your child's growth and development?"[3] It's
a sobering thought to realize that what we mean as "help" is
actually causing harm. But when you're parenting from your own
true identity, you know that *you* no longer have anything to
"prove" to anybody, and you want to pass that freedom along
to your kids. It won't be as simple as telling them not to work for
approval, but when you give them the freedom to be themselves
instead of miniature versions of you, it will go a long way toward
helping them find their own true identity.

I hope you can see that the idea behind this entire chapter is
that if you don't know who you really are, you're much more
likely to pass that sort of approach on to your kids. If you're
constantly searching for your identity through success in any
number of fields—finances, relationships, work, attractiveness,
achievement, fitness, etc.—then you will (even unintentionally)
teach your kids to look for their identity in those places, too.
Because if we're not feeling fulfilled by the thing that we're pursuing for fulfillment, we tend to think that *more* of that thing
will do it for us! (And I'm not writing this as somebody who is
above and beyond this challenge.)

By nature, I'm a very nostalgic person. We have photos and
small keepsakes from both my parents and grandparents and
Jane's featured prominently on a hanging fixture. Right below
this fixture, we have an old butter churn that my grandmother

---

[3] Paul David Tripp, *Parenting* (Wheaton, IL: Crossway, 2016), 81.

used to use. I like being able to show my grandkids a tangible piece of our family history. They've never seen anything like it, so they think it's neat just because it's so unique, and of course, there is a major emotional connection for me. But my nostalgia also shows up in a desire to collect. We still have most of the dolls, action figures, accessories, and books that our kids played with as they were growing up. It's ended up working out, because now all the grandkids play with them and are constantly asking all of us adults to help them identify obscure, thirty-year-old toys from *Teenage Mutant Ninja Turtles* and a wide range of other Saturday morning cartoons. But we didn't really save them in hopes that the grandkids would play with them; we saved them because I like to collect and hang on to stuff.

But I don't think you're getting the picture here. At my house, you can find old Pogs (remember those little paper milk caps that kids loved for a year or two in the '90s?), old magazines, old Barbies, old video game systems—pretty much anything old, but not old enough to be collectible or valuable! I have an emotional connection to that stuff, so I like to hang on to it. But I also proactively like to collect basketball cards. Kevin Durant is my favorite current NBA player and Michael Jordan is my all-time favorite (he's a lot better than LeBron, by the way). I sometimes notice myself searching for a card that I really want to add to my collection. First, I'll put it on my eBay watchlist. Then I'll try to figure out how to save up or trade to get it. And I'd be lying if I said I never think, *If I can get this card, that will feel so satisfying.*

I don't buy all of the cards I dream about—there are a lot of Michael Jordan cards that are really expensive! But when I do get the ones I want, the anticipation is almost greater than the excitement of actually holding the card in my hand. Before I get it, I can watch the tracking information and see it go from one shipping checkpoint to the next. Then I will finally get the beautiful update that it's "out for delivery." When I get home later that day, I'll grab the bubble mailer and rip it open so I can finally get a look at this card that I've been waiting for! I'll hold it up and look at it as I enjoy the satisfaction of having acquired something that I love so much. But after enjoying that "fulfillment" for a while (maybe thirty seconds to a minute!), I'll put it in the box where I keep my cards. Usually, not even a full day goes by before I start looking at the rest of that eBay watchlist and telling myself that the *next* card I get will be the one that will bring longer-lasting contentment.

I am fully aware that this description of my process sounds a whole lot like what kids do on Christmas morning—and what adults laugh about them doing. I'm excited about the "gift." Then I get what I was dreaming of, but I find that the "joy" it brings is actually just very short-term enjoyment. I need to keep reminding myself that having my little collections of different things is all fine and good, but if I ever find myself thinking that acquiring that *one* right thing will bring deep satisfaction, I'm chasing the wind. And I need to check that attitude in myself to make sure I'm not teaching my kids or grandkids (even accidentally and without knowing it) that the pursuit and acquisition of "stuff" has the ability to bring joy. Because it absolutely doesn't. I know it doesn't, and you know it doesn't. But I think it's also true that deep down, a little part of me thinks that maybe it does. And what I know about myself is that if I lose sight of the truth that my identity is found in Christ, there's a good chance I will accidentally teach my kids that "stuff" has the potential to satisfy.

It's not fun to think through how this shows up in your own life. Trust me, I just did it for a couple of pages and I don't love what I'm seeing there! But we need to do it, because ignoring our tendencies to find our identity or satisfaction in anything other than God is essentially setting ourselves up to pass some of these unhelpful and unhealthy approaches on to our kids. They will be able to see how we live our lives, and they will be able to tell where our priorities *actually lie*—not just where we say they do. I know this is a pretty strong and "in your face" challenge. But I'm making this point so strongly because of how important it is. Our kids need us to model healthy attitudes and behaviors so they can pattern their own attitudes and behaviors on them.

This topic bleeds into so many of the other chapters through this book. How you understand yourself in light of your sexuality impacts how you parent. How you understand yourself in light of your relationship with technology impacts how you parent. How you understand yourself in light of your interpersonal relationships impacts how you parent. In other words, we don't approach each parenting challenge with a blank mental slate; we bring our own pain, grief, and baggage to many of the things we're seeing our kids struggle with. And because of that, we may find that we're *reacting* rather than *responding* to some of those situations.

But when we find our true identity in God, we can let go of some of those other things. As we pursue God, we will find that we naturally deprioritize some of the things in which we used to find our identity. That is why spiritual practices like prayer, reading Scripture, and listening to God are so vital. They help us to keep things in the right perspective. And when we have our priorities in order, we are much more likely to set our kids up to do the same!

CHAPTER 2

PARENTING A CHILD WITH MENTAL HEALTH CONCERNS

Dan Seaborn and Dr. Emilie DeYoung

One of the silver linings of the COVID-19 pandemic is that mental health issues have taken center stage in the public arena. You've probably seen the mental and emotional toll it's taken in your own life as well as in those of your friends and coworkers—and you've undoubtedly noticed that kids and teens also are really struggling with loneliness, isolation, fatigue, worry, and occasionally, thoughts of harming or killing themselves. Some of those symptoms may be confusing, while others are downright scary. Parenting kids who are navigating mental health issues can be exhausting and can leave us feeling helpless.

Dr. Emilie DeYoung heads our division of Child and Adolescent Therapy at Winning At Home. She started this department and has been leading it since 2005. This chapter will focus on some of the things that Dr. Emilie consistently sees kids and parents struggling to work through together. She's been seeing children, adolescents, and families for more than twenty-five years and has some great wisdom to pass along to the rest of us.

The Big Two

There are several mental health issues that kids could be struggling with, but by far the two most common are anxiety and depression. If you have never experienced these issues or journeyed with a loved one who has, you may be unfamiliar with the specifics of how this plays out in a person's life.

Depression

Kids who suffer from depression may not come right out and say, "I'm depressed." That might be because they don't know how you'll react, but it might also be because they aren't able to put that fine of a point on their experience for themselves. Because it might not be something that they explicitly communicate, it's important to watch for patterns in their behavior that offer clues to what's going on inside.

Several behaviors can give a hint that your teen is struggling with depression. Teens with depression are persistently sad or hopeless—most of the day, nearly every day. They may spend excessive amounts of time isolated in their bedroom or have sudden changes in their demeanor (e.g., becoming more irritable or angry). They may use a lot of negative self-talk or have a persistent negative outlook no matter the situation. They may have a fascination with death or a lack of interest in things that they once enjoyed. They may be fatigued, sleep excessively, or have no interest in social opportunities. They may also struggle with appetite changes; they might snack or eat to excess, or they may have no appetite at all. Depression can also result in difficulty concentrating or making decisions. While all teenagers experience mood swings, those who experience depression show these behaviors consistently over longer periods (two weeks or more).

Lots of the behaviors listed above can have explanations other than depression, so don't start immediately diagnosing your introverted child as depressed because she likes to spend time in her bedroom. And don't immediately assume self-deprecating humor means depression, either. But if you see some of these symptoms showing up and you can't figure out what's going on, it would be wise to schedule a visit with a doctor or therapist to get some insight into what your child is going through.

I (Dan) would like to add an additional reminder here. I'm a pastor, not a mental health professional. People come to me looking for guidance and advice, but it's important that I understand the fields where I am equipped to offer help and the fields where I am not. When issues are related to mental health, diagnosing things, or other questions that are outside of my scope of training and expertise, I step back and communicate my limits. I mention this because I want to make it clear that there is a difference between areas where the answer is spiritually based and areas where something else needs to be addressed by a professional. In the same way that I don't set broken bones, I don't attempt to diagnose or treat mental health issues. Of course, I can offer advice and input about developing some healthy habits, but I can't provide comprehensive care. Having said that, I also remind our counseling and coaching team on a regular basis that their training is amazing and very necessary, but it doesn't mean they can stop relying on God. I encourage our counselors and coaches to start every session by praying and asking for God to move and work during their time with their clients. This is a nuanced discussion, but I wanted to make it clear that both a faith-only approach or a psychology-only approach will fall short of meeting all the needs of a kid who is struggling with his or her mental health.

Anxiety

Though some of the symptoms overlap, anxiety can look very different from depression. The hallmark of anxiety is excessive worry. While it might be difficult to notice as you're looking on from the outside, anxious brains often race as they think through potential outcomes and circumstances. The question that drives a lot of anxious thought is, "What if?" If you're not an anxious person, you probably think of those two words as offering a world of exciting possibilities. But for anxious people, they often point to a near-limitless number of possibilities of how things could go wrong. *What if I accidentally say something embarrassing or offensive? What if I can't do it? What if I take a risk and everything goes wrong all at once? What if there's something I'm not considering that is going to come back to bite me?* Those questions are general, but anxious brains are very adept at filling those questions in with all kinds of specific, detailed, and horrible potential issues and outcomes.

Kids and teens with anxiety can often appear distracted or easily embarrassed. It's common for them to experience sleep disturbance or appetite changes. Often, fears can paralyze them, resulting in things like refusing to go to school or throwing temper tantrums. Common fears of anxious kids include getting sick or vomiting, being trapped or going crazy, or being rejected by friends. As with depression, one or two of these symptoms don't guarantee a diagnosis, so follow up with a doctor or therapist if you think your child is dealing with anxiety.

If you don't experience anxiety but your child does, it can be incredibly challenging to understand what they may be going through. That's made even more complicated by the fact that it doesn't show up for everybody in the same way. For some, it's a sense of impending dread. For others, it's a constant worry about the way people perceive them. For still others, it's jumpiness and being easily startled. In his book *12 Rules for Life*, Dr. Jordan Peterson does a great job of describing a more severe way that anxiety shows up—a panic attack:

Her heart rate rises. She begins to breathe shallowly and quickly. She feels her heart racing and begins to wonder if she is suffering a heart attack. This thought triggers more anxiety. She breathes even more shallowly, increasing the levels of carbon dioxide in her blood. Her heart rate increases again, because of her additional fear. She detects that, and her heart rate rises again.

Poof! Positive feedback loop. Soon the anxiety transforms into panic, regulated by a different brain system, designed for the severest of threats, which can be triggered by too much fear. She is overwhelmed by her symptoms...[1]

If that seems like something your child has experienced, just know that they (and you) are not alone! Hopefully, seeing this description of the way anxiety can alarm people when they're experiencing normal physical sensations helps you realize that your child or teen is not artificially amplifying their experience to "get out of things." Serious anxiety and panic attacks are often "treatable" rather than "curable," but it will be helpful for your child to work through those options with a trained professional.

For parents who haven't experienced anxiety, depression, or any other form of mental health concern, it's important for you

---

[1] Jordan Peterson, *12 Rules for Life* (Toronto: Random House Canada, 2018), 21.

to remember that even if you can't *relate* to your kids, you can still be there for them. You might not know what to do or what they need from you. You definitely won't do it perfectly, but it will be immensely helpful for them to know that you want to do what you can to support them, and that you're not rolling your eyes whenever they describe their mental health concerns.

Whether your child is facing anxiety, depression, or something like obsessive compulsive disorder, post-traumatic stress disorder, eating disorders, or anything else, there are some things you can do and say that will be immediately helpful and others that will be immediately harmful. Let's start with a few to avoid:

Don't invalidate mental health.

Teen and child mental health issues are as real as physical health issues like acne. If your child demonstrates mental health issues, it is important to take them seriously. You wouldn't avoid taking him to the eye doctor if he were struggling with his vision. Take that same approach when it comes to his mental health, because whether he needs medication or to learn some skills to manage his symptoms, treatment can make a big difference. Also, if you take your child's mental health issues seriously, he is more likely to do the same. And we all know from personal experience that we can't grow in areas where we never acknowledge an issue in the first place. Minimizing the importance of mental health will almost assuredly cause more harm than good.

Don't tell them to "get over it."

While kids and teens are developing and learning, suggesting that they can "get over it" minimizes their negative experiences and conveys deep misunderstanding about what it feels like to live through something. This perpetuates negative feelings and fears, and often closes the door to further communication on the subject because they won't expect to feel heard or validated if they share their struggles with you. Adults sometimes want to apply the long view to what their kids are going through and tell them something like, "You won't even remember this in a couple of years." We say it in an attempt to be helpful and put things into perspective for them. And, honestly, that might even be true. But it isn't helpful, because they're living through it right now. With the benefit of hindsight, you probably remember your broken arm or first heartbreak or being bullied as "not that bad." But if we could go back in time and ask you about each of those experiences *while* you were experiencing them, your outlook would be a whole lot bleaker than it is when you think back on those moments years and years after the fact. Don't try to fast-forward through what your kids are going through. Instead, be there for them and sit with them in their pain and frustration.

Don't share the things they confide in you.

Adolescents are often becoming more aware of how other people perceive them, and they're also becoming more sensitive to those perceptions. Sharing their concerns with other parents or friends sabotages trust, and will likely result in them not sharing as freely the next time they have something they would like to talk to you about. Even if you are very open about all your own struggles, fears, and failures, you are not the one who should be deciding that your children's struggles, fears, and failures are an open book for the people around them to know about. When things that your kids expected to remain private are exposed to others (even if you don't see why it's a big deal), it can seriously harm their ability to trust you. This is also important because the things they shared with you are part of *their* story. And that is significant because when they choose to share their story in their own timeframe, it can be a powerful therapeutic step for them. The process of opening up about what they're dealing with will help them gain confidence and learn how to express themselves.

Don't suggest that they simply need stronger faith.

Mental health issues are often related to chemical imbalances that need to be treated from a holistic perspective that includes body, mind, and soul. Making statements that eliminate two important parts of this equation can leave young people feeling defeated and lost. It's actually more likely to cause harm than anything else, because now they may start feeling guilt, shame, or inadequacy *in addition* to whatever they were already struggling with. In fact, they will likely start thinking that not only are they struggling in the realm of mental health, they're also obviously not being obedient to God because they continue to struggle. That's a formula for a lot of hurt and disappointment. In situations where people feel that even their best isn't good enough, they often make the conscious effort to stop trying to do the right thing and start acting out because it's "what people expect" of them anyway. Try to put yourself in that scenario. If you were told that your issue was exclusively spiritual and you knew you were turning it fully over to God and you were doing your best to pursue Him, it would be really discouraging if things didn't improve. You might even start to question whether God cared or wanted to be involved in your life in the first place.

That is not an all-inclusive list, but it covers the biggest and most common mistakes that I (Emilie) see parents make as they navigate mental health concerns with their kids. Obviously, being there for your kids as they deal with challenges involves a lot more than just avoiding certain behaviors and perspectives. As you cut out those unhelpful approaches, here are some things to keep (or start) doing:

Develop empathy in your relationship.

Empathy involves putting yourself in your child's position. Don't imagine that forty-year-old you is facing the situation your child is facing. Instead, try to enter her world and understand how she's feeling and *why* that matters so much. Do your best to remember what it felt like to be rejected by your crush or to fail a test you had worked so hard to prepare for. Try to remember how it felt to be socially isolated or picked on. You can improve at this by practicing active listening. And while you're listening, resist the urge to jump in to "fix" the problem. Give your child space to participate in the problem-solving process. It's also important that you continue to show interest in what your kids are enduring and that you validate their concerns. Even if what they're facing wouldn't have bothered you when you were their age, realize that it *does* bother them, so it's important for you to be there for them as they figure it out. Doing that will continue to provide a safe space for these types of emotional conversations.

Ask hard questions!

For some reason, people naturally tend to think that if we don't acknowledge something, then it will eventually go away—and we can hold on to that belief despite all evidence to the contrary. When it comes to your child's mental health, avoidance is not a helpful option! Not talking about it will only serve to compound the problem, and it also will leave our kids feeling alone and isolated in the midst of their struggles. It is often helpful to check in with them by asking questions like, "Are you doing okay? You seem discouraged." Or "Are you feeling worried or stressed about this?"

But it's important to understand that questions with this level of depth will require that you have a good rapport with your child and that you have an open and trust-based relationship. Conversations can (or maybe should) start with small talk about their interests. If you're struggling to make headway as you build up to the more serious subject, you can talk to them about hairstyles, movies, or food. Finding some shared interests and focusing on them with small talk can help build the relational foundation that is needed to ask the harder questions. Developing language related to mental health and discussing these issues regularly helps make it normal to have conversations about mental and emotional health. That's important because then your kids will know you don't expect them to suffer in silence; they have a willing conversation partner in you.

Become an advocate for your child.

Treating mental health issues often requires services from primary care doctors, pastors, counselors, or psychotherapists. Kids and teens need adults who can help them navigate the mental health care system. It might take some extra work to find a provider that your insurance will cover, and the mental health professionals in your area are probably extremely busy right now so it may take some time to get an appointment. But you can show solidarity with your child by being the one to navigate that process for them (or with them, if they are old enough). This also involves making and keeping appointments with professionals who can help. It might strike you as odd, but our counseling and coaching providers have clients who fail to show up without calling to cancel their appointments on a surprisingly regular basis. We don't track that number specifically, but it happens enough to make it worth mentioning that simply making the appointment is not enough—you also need to keep it!

Find a mentor.

Especially during the teen years, kids can greatly benefit from conversations with adults who are not their parents. These adults could be teachers, pastors, therapists, grandparents, aunts or uncles, parents of some of their friends, or any number of other people. As long as it's an adult whom you trust will have your teen's best interests at heart and who will guide them in healthy ways, this is a great way to set your kids up for success. In fact, some research suggests that teens need at least five healthy adult relationships in their lives to navigate the journey to adulthood successfully. For more about how Jane and I (Dan) surrounded our kids with adults we trusted to mentor them well, see "It Takes a Team" (Chapter 7).

Promote healthy habits in the family environment.

As a parent, it's important that you model healthy coping skills. Kids and teens often "absorb" whatever emotion is prevalent in the home. If you lose your temper when you're feeling overwhelmed, that will feel like "normal" behavior to your kids. Instead of taking that approach (even if that's what was modeled for you when you were growing up), let your kids see you use things like exercise or meditation to relieve stress. It won't look the same for everybody, but we can all find ways to decompress. You could go for a walk in the woods, play or listen to music, or talk about what you're dealing with and feeling. You could throw a football or kick a soccer ball around, draw or paint something, or engage in some other hobby that you enjoy. When we find healthy ways to manage our own emotions, we're not just putting ourselves in a healthier position, we're also showing our kids some ways to potentially do that for themselves. Even when we might think they're not paying attention, our kids are constantly taking in information about the world around them. And when we model healthy coping strategies by practicing them ourselves, we're teaching them a lot more than we ever would by sitting them down and telling them how they should handle a particular situation. The example we set by taking care of our own mental health will encourage our kids to do the same for themselves.

Practical Coping Skills

I (Emilie) often train young people and parents to use a strategy I call Peanut Butter Pie. For me, thinking of peanut butter pie reminds me of Thanksgiving Day celebrations that I enjoyed with my extended family when I was a kid. Perhaps my favorite part of the day was the time when my grandma or mom would begin cutting the pie. I always enjoyed those pies—they were piled high with whipped cream, drizzled with chocolate, and loaded with flavor. Because it's such a fond memory, it helps me start from a positive place as I work to manage stress. I've also found that this coping strategy with a strange-sounding name is both memorable and approachable for the kids and adolescents I work with. "Peanut Butter Pie" is also a simple acronym for a coping method that honors body, mind, and spirit.

Pause (Mind)

While our minds often race with anxieties or destructive thoughts, that doesn't always have to be the case. Although our brains are exceptionally good at rehashing the past or predicting the future (these can be positive or negative memories or projections), it's important that we learn to put our brains on "Pause" just like we can pause our music or videos. Once we pause, we can "change the channel" in our brains to more productive thinking. One way to do this would be to focus on a peaceful place and ask *What do I see? What do I hear? What do I smell? What do I taste? What do I feel?* It's important to remember that pausing opens up the possibility of breaking the cycle of these destructive thoughts. If there is no change in circumstances or behavior, it's unlikely that there will be an opportunity to transition from the anxious thought to another one. If an analogy helps here, imagine a car or truck stuck in mud or a snowbank. Continuing to try to step on the gas pedal harder and harder will not be the solution; in fact, that often makes the situation worse. Instead, you need to stop, put the vehicle in park, and go assess the situation. In the same way, pausing gives your child (and you too, if it's helpful) the opportunity to stop trying to think themselves out of a situation that is the result of overthinking. Simply thinking harder can't be the solution when it caused the problem in the first place.

While paused, there are some techniques that can help kids "detach" from the thought that was so engrossing. One way is the "Rainbow Technique." While the brain is paused, you can look around your environment to name something that is red, orange, yellow, etc. You could also count backwards from one hundred slowly, or think of a category (e.g., sports teams, vegetables, cars) and name as many things as you can think of that fit into it. While these approaches may seem really simple, they are actually quite effective. The important thing is to give the mind something else to focus on so you can stop fixating on the anxious thoughts.

Breathe (Body)

There are many tips that people find helpful when it comes to healthy breathing. The most important thing to remember is to take deep, slow breaths, as if you are blowing a bubble through a bubble wand. Taking several long, slow breaths in a row can promote a sense of peace and calmness. Counting in your head as you take each breath in and let each breath out can help provide a baseline to make sure that you're taking deep breaths.

It may strike you as a bit strange to think that changing your breathing pattern can have any kind of impact on your mental or emotional state, but it absolutely does! If you're skeptical and want to test this out before you pass it along to your child, give it a try now. You can start by making it your goal to count to five as you take a deep breath in and then count to five again as you blow it out. Or you may find that it's more helpful to focus on breathing out, because your body will naturally breathe in after a forced exhalation. Give it a try for a minute or so and see if you feel a sense of peace or calmness, even if there is activity around you. You may be surprised to find that it actually *is* helping you develop a sense of inner peace and calmness.

Mindful or intentional breathing is such a helpful tool because it's something you already have to do, which means it's possible to practice this anytime and anyplace anxiety strikes. It's just as effective when you're around other people as it is lying in bed at night—or during a big meeting at work or a big test at school.

There are many other "body" techniques that can be helpful, but we'll close this section with a couple that can be very effective in many different situations. One is "Butterfly Hugs." This practice is very simple—all you need to do is wrap your arms across your chest and gently tap your hands on your shoulders like the wings of a butterfly. Doing wall push-ups can also be very effective, especially when the anxiety is showing up in the form of body sensations. In the same way that thinking of something different can help move your mind away from fixating on the anxious thoughts, doing something physical can help stop unwanted body sensations.

Pray (Spirit)

When emotions are intense, it is helpful to turn worries or concerns into prayers. First Peter 5:7 tells us, "Cast all your anxiety on him because he cares for you." The sad irony is that if we think of this verse as a command that we are to follow instead of an invitation to turn anxieties over to our loving God, it can end up causing more anxiety. But we don't cast our anxieties on God because we *have* to, we do it because we *get* to! God cares about what is going on with us. Especially when we think sharing our fears, worries, and insecurities with another person will make us feel too vulnerable, God is always ready and willing to hear about those things. Jesus told His disciples that God knew the number of hairs on their heads (Luke 12:7) as a way to remind them of His deep care for and understanding of each of them. Knowing this, God isn't inviting us to tell Him about our worries and problems and fears because He's unaware of them; He's asking us to share them because He cares and wants to hear from us! In the same way that we talk through issues with our friends and loved ones, God has made Himself available to hear from us. There can be a lot of value in naming these fears and saying them out loud, because putting our thoughts and feelings into words can help us pinpoint how we're actually feeling in the first place. If it is a struggle to find the words to express the feelings, simply speaking the name of Jesus can be a great form of prayer and a way to begin the journey of turning our fears and anxieties over to Him.

In Closing

Almost everybody has their own unique story around their personal experience with mental health. But if you've never had any, it can be tempting to think that these issues are "all in somebody's head" or that "they just need to get over it because everybody feels sad sometimes." Just know that psychological study continues to reveal more and more about the importance of child and adolescent mental health as the field advances. If you're tempted to gloss over things, please reconsider that approach and take your children's mental health seriously.

Or maybe you are on the other end of the spectrum. Maybe you had some mental health issues yourself when you were younger, but you grew up in a home where those concerns were ignored or minimized. If that was the case for you, do your best to offer your kids a more supportive environment than the one you experienced. Give your kids the gift of care and support, and help them find the tools they need to thrive.

CHAPTER 3

HANDLING
TECHNOLOGY WELL

Dan Seaborn and Pastor Alan Seaborn

In large part, I'm going to turn this chapter over to my son, Alan. He's a pastor who works with me at Winning At Home and he's been speaking on the topic of technology and families since 2016. And more importantly, he's a whole lot younger than me, and knows about technology firsthand!

This content has been developed over the course of my (Alan's) speaking to parents and grandparents of children of all ages. I first started talking about technology for a local event that our county put on about fatherhood. And since I couldn't preach a sermon, I figured I was still young enough to have a good feel for technology, so I jumped in. Some of this information comes from talks I've done over the years; I've shared about it in podcast form as well as through the Kidmin App's email newsletter.

To set this chapter up, I want to share a brief funny interaction I had when I was sharing some of these ideas in a breakout session at a men's conference in the Midwest. During the Q&A time at the end of my talk, a man who I would guess was in his mid- to late sixties stood up and pulled his phone out of his pocket. He held it up high to present it to the rest of the group and said loudly, "This thing right here is the devil!" Before I could respond, the guy sitting next to him looked up at him and asked, "Then why do you have one in your pocket?" There was some laughter for a moment before the guy who was against phones sheepishly said, "Well, I need to have one for my work."

Thinking back, that's probably a pretty accurate depiction of how many people feel about their always-present devices. We love and hate them at the exact same time. We love them because of how convenient they make accessing information, staying in touch with loved ones, and driving to our destination without getting lost. But we hate them for giving us an outlet for our worst impulses. They let us keep a little private world which nobody, or very few people, can access. We can comment anonymously and let our anger out in secret, we can text or message people we shouldn't, and we can access content that doesn't make us better, more loving people. And that's without touching on the untold hours that we can easily waste without even realizing that we've just watched four episodes of our new show, or we've been scrolling so far down on our favorite app that we'd be embarrassed for anybody to find out just how long we'd spent.

Despite the downsides, I am very pro-technology, because when we use our devices appropriately, the world opens up to us in ways it never would otherwise. I lived in South Africa for twelve months during my college years, and video chats and email were my only connection to family and friends back home. It's been over a decade since then, and today those same technologies (and newer and better ones) allow me to stay connected to my South African friends in a way that would be impossible otherwise.

Even without the international element, there are so many benefits. I have a terrible sense of direction, so having my phone double as a GPS has been a game-changer for me. I'm a big NBA fan, so streaming games and being able to watch live coverage has kept me in the loop when I'm not able to be at home. And I haven't even mentioned the ability to call or text to stay connected.

Despite the negatives, our devices and today's technology go a long way toward keeping us connected, and they make things a lot more convenient. I'll be addressing some of the downsides at various points throughout this chapter, but first I want to give a little perspective on the difference between the way that most adults see the internet and technology compared to the way that kids and teens see it.

Bridging the Gap

The world is unbelievably different today than it was when I was growing up, and I'm only thirty-six! I remember getting an internet connection at home for the first time and having to wait until after 9 p.m. to go online with our dial-up connection so I wouldn't tie up our all-important home phone line. I remember (and I bet you do too) the jarring "eeeeeee-uuuuhhhhhhh, eeeeeee-uuuuuuuhhhh" sound of the family computer connecting to our dial-up internet. I also remember it taking me fifteen to twenty minutes to download a single song. That feels like an impossibly long time, doesn't it? But that's the world that I (and probably you) grew up in. As we seek to lead and guide kids with the proper boundaries around technology, we find ourselves unable to figure out how to best help them navigate the decisions they're having to make because we never faced them! If we need to help kids navigate a difficulty when it comes to friendships, relationships, school, or driving, we can fall back on our own life experiences. But when it comes to technology, our experiences and theirs likely have very little in common.

To help you remember just how different things were not that long ago, I remember telling my parents at age sixteen that I didn't want the cell phone they gave me because I was sure they only got it so they could keep tabs on me at all times! And on top of that, cell phones weren't actually that great back then. I would lose the signal driving down one of the main streets in my hometown. Text messages cost me twenty-five cents to send or receive. It wasn't a smooth or elegant thing.

Dr. Bradley Howell, the dean of Teaching and Learning at Gordon-Conwell Theological Seminary, shared a powerful example of the divide between the way parents and their kids often think of technology and the internet. In the internet's early days, it was often referred to as "the information superhighway." You don't hear that term used any more, but Dr. Howell writes that it may have shaped perspectives more than we know. In *Adoptive Youth Ministry*, he writes about how that impacts the way parents and kids view the internet:

> [P]arents who adopted this mental model of the internet as an information superhighway and a generation of young people who did not, this is a subtle but important distinction. The information age shaped the perspective of modern parents and their spiritual communities toward an internet that existed to give and receive information, but it was considered to be a virtual world—a shadow of the real thing—and socially isolating. That understanding of the internet is a far cry from the mental model that a new generation of internet adopters would soon take.[1]

That perspective is so helpful in explaining the disconnect between the way parents and kids often view technology. It can be hard for adults to imagine that online interactions with friends

---

[1] Chap Clark, ed., *Adoptive Youth Ministry* (Grand Rapids, MI: Baker Academic, 2016), 55.

are "real." And that makes sense if we're thinking of the internet as a "place" that's separate from the rest of life. But kids are growing up in a world where the internet has always existed, so they didn't need to create a mental category to fit it into.

Think of it this way: The things that are part of our lives when we're growing up are what we just think of as "normal." The style of communication and connection that was prevalent in your family just feels normal and right to you. The roles of each of the people in the family felt normal and right. It's only when you experience other approaches that you see the strengths and weaknesses of what seems "normal" to you. That's because what we grow up in and around is just what makes up life for each of us.

And that isn't just true when it comes to family dynamics. It's also true for the technology that existed when we were growing up. We don't think of mailing a letter or talking to somebody on the phone as being different from "real life." Kids who grow up with access to the internet view online connections in much the same way. That key idea can be really helpful for parents to understand, because it can help us to see the difference in the way we're viewing online interactions and the way our kids or grand-kids view them. Highlighting the different perspectives of kids and adults leads us right into the topic of addiction.

Addiction

When I (Alan) first looked into how many hours each day kids and teens are using technology, I was shocked. They use some form of screen time for an average of nine hours per day—that's a huge amount! But then I started thinking about my own screen time. I'm probably in front of a computer for six or so hours every day. I play music or a podcast while dinner is cooking, and then my wife and I sit on the couch and watch Netflix or browse on our phones. Often, I stay up to watch basketball after my wife goes to bed. It's not a stretch at all for me to get ten or eleven hours of screen time in a day. And that's not even counting the time I spend listening to music or podcasts.

The number of hours we spend with technology throughout the day is astounding. And I have a feeling that if we, as adults, would look at how prevalent screen time is in our own lives, we might better be able to understand just how fully integrated it is in our world today. If we can see that, we might better understand why kids spend so many hours connected to technology.

Of course, some forms of screen time are better and more valuable than others. When apps or websites are set up to allow infinite scrolling (in contrast to reaching the end of a page and having to click a link to see more results), the very design is set up to keep us scrolling down and down and down. When looking at the news or social media, it feels like it just keeps bringing us more frustration, anxiety, envy, and disappointment. If that's hard for us to manage as adults, just imagine how much more challenging it is for kids!

The term "addiction" is something we probably all feel like we understand well, but it's still important to break it down. Dr. Mark Griffiths, a professor of behavioral addiction in the United Kingdom, says he is often approached by parents who say their teenage sons are addicted to online gaming and their teenage daughters are addicted to social media. He tells them:

> This is simply a case of parents pathologizing their children's behavior because they think what they are doing is "a waste of time." I always ask parents the same three things in relation to their child's screen use. Does it affect their schoolwork? Does it affect their physical education? Does it affect their peer development and interaction?[2]

Notice that he doesn't ask "Do you wish your child spent more time on schoolwork?" Because that's a different question. He's encouraging us to ask if the technology itself is what's taking away from the time doing schoolwork or exercising or making friends. The genuine answer is often that kids are using screens in a similar way that adults are, to relax or to unplug during some downtime. But they also use technology to connect with friends in a way that is hard for adults to wrap their heads around. This is not to minimize the possibility of addiction, because apps, games, websites, and YouTube or TV channels are often designed intentionally to keep us engaged for as long as possible because they make money with every advertisement we see or click. Or they try to sell us in-game upgrades to improve our style or performance.

---

[2] Mark D. Griffiths, "Screenagers and Technology Use," *Psychology Today* (blog), August 24, 2016, https://www.psychologytoday.com/us/blog/in-excess /201608/screenagers-and-technology-use.

Of course, kids struggle with compulsively checking for messages, likes, or updates. But it's helpful to remember that adults struggle with compulsively checking for emails, responses, or deadlines that we're responsible for as well. When we can see that we and our kids both struggle in similar ways, it will help us to respond to them with empathy rather than annoyance and frustration.

It's easy to forget what we were like when we were younger, but my guess is that there were things you loved and did often that exasperated your parents. It may have been carrying a tattered toy or blanket around, focusing on one hobby or skill to the exclusion of almost everything else, or spending excessive time with friends. Remember what it felt like to have such tunnel vision about what mattered to you, and know that your kids are feeling those same things today about being able to stay connected with friends and followers online. This isn't a defense of kids going all-in on technology all the time, but I hope it reminds you that you most likely had similar tendencies your own parents may have handled in unproductive ways as well. Hopefully that will help you avoid making unannounced, sweeping changes, or proclamations that will do more harm than good!

Cyberbullying

While we're thinking back to our own adolescent and teen years, what kind of experiences did you have with bullies? It's very likely there was a person or two (or more) that you really didn't get along with when you were growing up. Maybe it was a neighbor or somebody at school. Maybe it was a sibling or somebody at church. You know the feeling, though: when you saw that specific person, you were immediately on edge, because you knew you had to be ready to defend yourself physically, emotionally, or verbally. Whether or not you would define those experiences as "bullying," you can certainly remember. Kids don't often realize what they're doing, and they don't often mean to cause harm to the people around them. But bullying has always been a fact of life. The big difference today is that bullies' access to their victims is no longer limited to the bus ride, the playground, or the moments when Mom or Dad aren't around.

Now, kids are reachable all the time. Negative comments can be made and received twenty-four hours a day, leaving kids vulnerable even in their own homes. One of the most significant steps that parents can take in helping their kids deal with cyberbullying (of themselves or others) is letting them know they won't get in trouble for reporting something to you. In fact, Dr. Pamela M. Anderson writes, "Young people realize that if they discuss problems with bullying and harassment, parents may close down their social media accounts, take away their phones, or otherwise restrict their access to the online social world."[3] Think about that statement. Kids may view being bullied as just "the cost" of being part of the world online. Although a quick scroll through a comment section on any news article will probably affirm that idea for each of us, it absolutely should not be the case! Let your

[3] Pamela M. Anderson, "Why Teens Don't Report Cyberbullying," *Youth Tech Health* (blog), August 2, 2017, https://yth.org/teens-dont-report-cyberbullying/.

kids know the best way to deal with negative comments online is to bring them to you and ask for help in resolving the issues.

It's one thing to assume that your kids could potentially be victims of cyberbullying, but few parents want to imagine their kids are the perpetrators. In *iRules*, Janell Burley Hofmann tells of a conversation she had with her son after he made a joking comment to a friend online. She asked him a few simple questions to help him see things from a different perspective: "Okay, would you have said that in front of her parents? What if her parents read it? How would you feel then?"[4] These simple questions can go a long way toward helping kids and teens understand that their words and actions impact others. It's a wonderful way to help them think things through on a deeper level and to increase their awareness of the weight of their words.

Many different organizations and websites have worked to create things like an Internet Code of Conduct or an Internet Safety Pledge that kids (and adults) commit to as they interact with others online. In its version of an Internet Safety Pledge, iKeepSafe.org includes these three ideas in a section on relationships:

- I am kind online and offline.
- I only share images of others with their consent.
- I take ten deep breaths before posting something when I feel angry or upset.[5]

---

[4] Janell Burley Hoffman, *iRules* (New York: Rodale, 2014), 25.
[5] "Internet Safety Pledge Level II," iKeepSafe, http://archive.ikeepsafe.org/wp-content/uploads/2016/04/Internet-Safety-Pledge-IIx.pdf.

I don't know about you, but I know many adults who would do well to commit to living up to these standards! As with most rules or standards, there will be missteps along the way. But it's important that your kids know what the expectations are so that they're not blindsided when you start enforcing your rules. You can create your own agreement for your family to use, or modify one that is already available.

Sexting

I (Alan) have shared on the topic of sexting in several places, in both church and non-religious settings. For the most part, parents were engaged and understood the seriousness of this issue when it comes to their kids. However, there are two responses I want to specifically address before moving forward. Some parents think that because their family takes faith seriously, this won't be an issue. Others may not really be sold on Christianity's view of sexual morality, and they may think the sexual ethics we talk about in the church are too restrictive.

Whether or not you think your kids may ever send or receive an explicit text, email, message, etc., you need to let them know it's something you feel very strongly about and that you want to protect them in this arena. The American Academy of Pediatrics put it best:

> Make sure kids of all ages know that it is not appropriate or smart to send or receive pictures of people

without clothing, or sexy text messages, no matter whether they are texting friends or strangers.[6]

That's about as straightforward as can be. But in addition to the emotional and spiritual harm that can result from those kinds of activities, there may also be legal ramifications. Laws around underaged sexting vary from state to state, but in Michigan (where Winning At Home is based), Kelly & Kelly Law explains the potential legal consequences of sexting:

1. Taking photographs of genitals, pubic area, buttocks, or female breasts that are of a person under the age of eighteen is child pornography, this includes taking photos of your own body. This is a 20-year felony.
2. Sending, reproducing, or distributing these photos is a 7-year felony.
3. Possession of sexually abusive material related to a minor is a 4-year felony.[7]

Regardless of whether you think sexual exploration is normal and to be expected, or if you think your children will

---

[6] American Pediatric Association, "How to Make a Family Media Use Plan," Healthychildren.org, updated November 30, 2020, https://www.healthychildr en.org/English/family-life/Media/Pages/How-to-Make-a-Family-Media -Use-Plan.aspx.
[7] "Michigan Sexting Laws—Crimes and Penalties," Kelly & Kelly P.C., https:// kellykellylaw.com/michigan-criminal-law/sexting-crimes/.

never run into a situation involving sending or receiving sexually explicit material, you really need to have this conversation with them. We're not talking about a difference of opinion on the best way to protect a child—we're talking about helping your children avoid making bad decisions that could have life-ruining consequences. Please, please have this conversation with your kids. Even if you feel awkward. Even if they feel awkward. Even if it makes them mad. You can blame it on this book or this chapter if you'd like—we don't care, we just want you to have the conversation! Because, as adults, it's our job to help protect kids—especially in areas where they don't want to be protected!

Which Apps Are Okay?

As I (Alan) make presentations on technology and talk with parents about the opportunities and risks that come along with it, many ask me about the appropriateness of different apps for their kids at different ages, or at what age it's appropriate to give a child his own cell phone. As you can imagine, those are loaded questions. Each family is different (and each kid in each family is different!), and what one parent thinks is fine for their child may offend someone else.

My recommendation is always to defer to the parents to make that decision, but in an informed way. That's not a copout, although I understand it might feel that way at first. But think about it for a moment. If your kids are older, think back on how different their maturity levels were when each of them were eight or twelve or sixteen. With some of your kids, you were less anxious than with others as you sent them off to camp or let them drive alone for the first time. But nearly all parents have felt that extra level of anxiety when they started loosening the restrictions on at least one of their kids—most likely because they knew the temperament and strengths and weaknesses of each of their individual children. Having said that, it's also very possible that they were surprised by the outcomes along the way. Maybe the most mature and responsible child acted out at school or camp in a way that they never would have expected. Maybe their wild child thrived in that type of setting. Figuring out when you're comfortable letting your kids have access to certain devices or apps is the same. You might be convinced that one of your kids can or can't handle the added responsibility, and you may or may not be right. Some of this will certainly be trial and error. You'll give your kids the opportunity to succeed and gain freedom or fail and then have to spend more time learning how to handle it responsibly.

It's important to remember this is a learning process and a journey. It's probably fair to say most of the people reading this had some kind of car accident as they were learning how to drive. That's why new drivers usually spend most of their time behind the wheel of older (and less than pristine) cars.

When my dad was teaching me to drive a manual transmission, we went to a big, empty church parking lot. I was practicing backing up when I ran into the cement foundation of a light pole.

As you can imagine, the pole took no damage, but the bumper on the car I had spent all my money to buy did! But that wasn't a reason for my dad to say that I was a failure at driving and it was time to take the keys away. He just knew it meant we needed to spend more time on backing up, using mirrors, and having better situational awareness. In the same way, an online misstep doesn't necessarily mean it's time to take extreme action with your child, either. It might just mean it's time to revisit the ideas of treating people kindly, of avoiding violent, explicit, or age-inappropriate content, or of limiting or eliminating unsupervised internet access.

Again, remember that this isn't just a new challenge for you and your kids to navigate. This is a new struggle *every* parent and child is learning how to navigate. Pervasive device use and internet access is a very recent development in human history, so be gracious with yourself as you learn how to handle the challenges it presents. Unlike most things in life, we don't have access to wisdom from history or from our elders to lean on here.

Instead of writing a paragraph each about a few key apps that kids and teens are using right now (which would be completely out of date and useless in six months), we want to empower you to learn more about the positives and negatives of whatever app you need to learn about. Common Sense Media (commonsensemedia.org) offers unbiased reviews and explanations of apps, including one-minute video overviews of what many apps are for and why kids like them, as well as recommendations for which ages the apps are appropriate for. This is a great tool for helping parents understand which apps their kids are using and to make informed decisions about what they are comfortable with letting their kids access. In the many hours that I've spent researching this topic, commonsensemedia.org is the best resource I have come across. It saves parents from having to start from scratch each time a new app is downloaded, and it helps them get up to speed very quickly.

This chapter also needs to include at least a brief section about devices in bedrooms at night. Many of us probably struggle with the continual distraction that our phones can create if we leave them plugged in and sitting on our nightstands. It's just too tempting to grab our handheld world-exploring device when we aren't falling asleep immediately. Or to check that text, email, or message when we wake up at 3 a.m. If we struggle to control those impulses as adults, how much harder must it be for kids—who already aren't really known for being able to control their impulses! That's why many child development experts recommend having a "family charging station" for devices located somewhere in a common area. If phones stay out of the bedroom at night, you're taking one more step to set your kids up for a successful night of sleep. And the best way to make this a practice that sticks is to lead by example. Let your kids know it's hard for you too, but it's just better for none of you to have the phone next to you all night. Not only is it an on-demand distraction, health concerns are emerging over how the "blue light" emitted by our devices signals our bodies to stop producing melatonin, which is a hormone that helps regulate sleep and wake cycles, because blue light is what the sun creates during the day. Our devices are actually telling our bodies that it's not time to sleep![8]

Also, if kids have devices in their room at night, they have completely unsupervised time with them. Although we had both explicit-content blocking set up on our wireless router as well as accountability software on the family computer, as a teenager I (Alan) was able to find loopholes in both with enough trial and error when I was on the computer after everybody else had gone to sleep. No matter what steps you put in place, your kids will most likely work to undermine them. Not because they are especially devious or bad, but because that's what kids do! So work to protect them from their worst impulses and create a charging station in the living room or dining room.

All these issues are complicated and challenging to navigate as a family. There won't be a single solution that will work for everybody. But if you can work to identify an Internet Code of Conduct or something similar for your family, it should address all these topics and lay out clear expectations. That doesn't mean there won't be tweaks over time, but it's important to know what the rules and standards are in order to keep everybody on the same page and to set your kids up for success when it comes to technology.

---

[8] Anya Kamenetz, *The Art of Screen Time* (New York: Public Affairs, 2018), 22–23.

CHAPTER 4

PARENTING IN A HYPERSEXUALIZED WORLD

Dan Seaborn and Coach Brad Klaver

This chapter is unique in the sense that very few (if any) parents need to be convinced of the importance of this information. In conversations about technology, mental health, or social skills, there can easily be different viewpoints that lead parents not to worry too much about how they navigate a specific issue. But this one hits close to home for everybody. With casual and recreational sex being part of so many TV and movie plots, song lyrics, and general discussions in media and online, our kids are getting a very different message from the world than the one they are getting from us, our churches, and from Scripture.

Trying to discuss God's view of sex amidst the constant background noise celebrating free sexual expression and championing hookup culture can certainly feel like a losing battle. But in this chapter, we will address a scriptural view of sexuality and talk about how our perspective as parents will help shape the way our kids think of sex.

Obviously, addressing how sexuality is approached throughout Scripture is a huge topic. Entire books have been written about this, so trying to reduce it to a single chapter means it'll have to be a brief overview. In many ways, this chapter can either stand alone, or be read along with the next one, "Gender and Sexuality," which will focus specifically on sexual orientation and gender identity from a Christian perspective.

A Christian Sexual Ethic

Consistency in how we approach sexuality and gender with our view of Scripture is key. As in so many other areas of parenting, it's easy to *react* rather than *respond* when we're anxious, worried, or afraid of what our kids might be doing. Those reactionary conversations rarely accomplish much besides creating conflict between us and our kids. That's why it's key that our views and expectations around healthy sexuality are part of a bigger, fuller approach to our view of all humanity. A "Christian sexual ethic" is the agreed-upon terminology to describe this view. A Christian sexual ethic focuses on historical, orthodox, long-held perspectives on sexuality and gender. We believe our view on sex and sexuality has to be couched within the larger biblical story, and it has to be seen through the lens of the nature of the relationship between God and humanity. This requires us to ask, "Are we made for ourselves, or are we made for intimacy with our Creator?" Our modern world gives us one answer. But our faith gives us a different one.

Writing about a Christian sexual ethic is impossible without first focusing on the importance of submission and surrender to God. The way sexuality intersects with Christianity must fall under the umbrella of Christianity itself. And that is why we must start with surrender. Surrender, repentance, and letting go of our attempts to control are all at the core of what it looks like to be faithful to God. This seems completely obvious when you read it written out like that, but stop and think about it for a moment. Our culture is constantly sending us messages about sexuality that fly in the face of any kind of surrender to God: "What happens between two consenting adults isn't wrong." "Looking isn't touching." "Porn use is the result of a healthy sexual appetite." "Bachelor parties require strippers." "Teens should experiment; it's healthy." And those are only a few of the messages we all hear on a regular basis from our culture and society. The perspective behind all those ideas is that it's fine to do what you want as long as you're not hurting anybody else. Or, more accurately, as long as you don't obviously see the hurt you are causing.

But as Christians, on topics where the Bible speaks, we don't take our cues on right and wrong from culture or from the viewpoint of the average American. We don't decide what is right and wrong based on public sentiment. What it means to follow Jesus is to make Him Lord of our lives. In fact, part of the reason that "Jesus is Lord" was a saying among early Christians is because the phrase of their dominant culture was "Caesar is lord." In their beautifully titled book *Jesus Is Lord, Caesar Is Not*, Scot McKnight and Joseph B. Modica write:

> A simple reading of Luke 2 reveals Luke using the following terms for Jesus—*Savior* and *Lord*, and alongside those terms are the terms *gospel* (good news) and *peace*. Now it so happens . . . that these are the precise terms used of Caesar in Rome, the very terms broadcast throughout the empire on declarations and in letters and on countless inscriptions visible in all major cities in the empire . . . His words were laced with criticism of Rome—to say Jesus was Lord and Savior or to say Jesus was the one who brings peace and is good news is at the same time, in a covert way, to say Caesar was not Lord and not Savior, and that his good news and peace ring hollow.[1]

We no longer have a single figurehead called "lord," but it would not be a stretch at all to say we're living in a time where

---

[1] Scot McKnight and Joseph B. Modica, *Jesus Is Lord, Caesar Is Not* (Downers Grove, IL: InterVarsity Press, 2013), 16.

we could replace the word *Caesar* with *culture, public sentiment,* or *politics.* So how this translates to our current reality is that if "Jesus is Lord," then culture or politics or public sentiment is not. And *that's* good news. We're all feeling burned out from living in a world that tried to make each of those things the supreme form of knowledge or truth. From personal experience, we know it doesn't work. Instead of being uplifted by placing any of those things as the guiding principle of our country, we have seen division, hatred, and anger reign.

One of the foundational components of an understanding of Christian sexual ethics is that if we submit to the lordship of Jesus, then our American perspective of seeing the world through the lens of our "rights" quickly fails us. Because what God calls us to is a life of surrender. A life of giving up. A life of letting go. Those sound a lot less like rights and more like responsibility. The responsibility that we have is to change in order to live in alignment with His lordship.

In one of the great early hymns or poems of the church, Paul writes this about Jesus in Philippians 2:6–8.

> Who, being in very nature God,
> did not consider equality with God something to be
> used to his own advantage;
> rather, he made himself nothing
> by taking the very nature of a servant,
> being made in human likeness.
> And being found in appearance as a man,

he humbled himself
by becoming obedient to death—
even death on a cross!

This passage lays out the journey that Jesus took of denying Himself and letting go of His rights in order to fulfill a bigger purpose than His own temporary comfort or happiness. Our invitation is to be His followers and to make him lord of our lives. And if our Lord modeled letting go and giving of Himself, we don't have the option to do the opposite and yet say we're being faithful in following Him. If we continue to apply our individualistic perspective and think in terms of "rights" rather than "responsibilities," we see that we are essentially setting ourselves up to fall short of God's calling.

The very core of our existence is the fact that we're made for communion and relationship with God. Augustine wrote in Book I of his *Confessions*, "You have made us for yourself and restless is our heart until it comes to rest in you."[2] That quote may already be familiar to some of you; the reason it's been able to stay in the public consciousness 1,600 years after Augustine wrote it is because it rings true for people century after century. His words, of course, echo what we see throughout Scripture. The Bible has a consistent story throughout: God's pursuit of a relationship with His people.

Sometimes we see this pursuit from God's perspective and sometimes we see it from people's. God leads Israel out of Egypt,

---

[2] Saint Augustine, *Confessions* (New York: Barnes and Noble Classics, 2007), 3.

into the desert, and ultimately into the Promised Land. The Psalmist in Psalm 91 calls God "my refuge and my fortress" and in Psalm 42 writes that he longs for God "as the deer pants for streams of water." Zacchaeus climbed a tree to catch a glimpse of Jesus (Luke 19). In John 4, Jesus talks to the woman at the well and tells her that he has spiritual "water" that actually satisfies. All these stories and moments point to relationship and pursuit.

But even though we all know what it takes to be in relationship with somebody and what it looks like to pursue that, for some reason, when it comes to our relationship with God, we tend to approach it differently. In fact, you've probably heard somebody ask a question along the lines of, "What's okay for me to do that won't break this relationship?" Think about the perspective that often leads to this question: "Is God okay with _____?" Instead, the helpful question is to ask what we can do in order to draw closer to God and to live in closer alignment to His standards for us. We don't often think in terms of what we can get away with when it comes to our other relationships. We don't think, *What's the furthest I can go in hurting my spouse without breaking up my marriage?* Or, *How far past the line can my comments or actions go before this person stops being my friend?* Or, *How much pain can I expose my children to and still have a relationship with them when they get older?* We don't think in those terms because we understand that marriage, parenting, and friendship all fall into the category of relationships, and we have a good idea of what will be helpful and what will be harmful to a relationship. But when we start asking, "How much is God willing to forgive if I don't live according to His standards?" we're missing the point. We're moving our connection with God into some category other than relationship—more like a transaction or a business deal. If we approach it with that perspective, we're viewing it more as an obligation than a relationship.

This is what happens when we make our sexuality and gender identity the central part of our lives: we're moving away from the picture of the relationship between God and humanity. In Genesis, we see God and His creation walking together, naked in the Garden of Eden. This is a picture of unbroken access and relationship. After Adam and Eve's disobedience, when God comes to visit them in the garden (and they hide when they hear Him coming), before He does anything else, God asks a question that centers around connection and relationship. He calls out to Adam and asks, "Where are you?" (Genesis 3:9). That is a small detail in the story that most of us have probably missed, because we think of the Fall as a story of punishment and judgment. But it's important to note that God starts with an effort to stay connected before He moves into condemnation. His deepest desire for each of us is to be in right relationship with Him, and He calls us to that again and again.

It's not immediately obvious, but unhealthy sexual behavior actually seems to be rooted in this desire for deep connection. Our modern culture gets it backward and tends to think of sex as the great connector rather than the healthy expression that comes out of a deep and lifelong commitment—and a firm connection to other people is our deep longing. We all want to be made whole; to have a profound and abiding connection with others. As Christians, we know that this longing can only find fulfillment by being made whole in a relationship with God. But far, far more people seek to create that connection with other people, often with painful and unfortunate results.

(Slightly) Reframing Marriage

When it comes time to talk about this with our children, here's how I (Brad) approach it. In many ways, we've made marriage itself the target. Stop and think about it for a moment: we truly do live in a culture (especially the Christian community) where marriage has become the ultimate goal. Ask single young adults about their experience when they go to church or family gatherings. Most, if not all, of them will report having been asked about their romantic life in less than delicate ways. "Do you think you'll *ever* get married?" "Don't you want kids? If you do, it's time to get moving on finding a spouse!" "One of my friends has a daughter around your age…"

While these questions and comments come from well-meaning people who undoubtedly have good intentions, they do serve to drive home the point that a late-twenty-something or thirty-something single person is "less than" or "missing out" if they aren't married. Again, the comments come from a good place. The person asking these kinds of questions is often communicating that they are glad to be married, so they want this good thing to happen for the person they're talking to as well. And there's nothing wrong with that idea at all. But it can contribute to elevating *marriage itself* to the highest state somebody can attain—and that doesn't reflect a Christian sexual ethic.

The ultimate longing of our hearts is to find fulfillment. That fulfillment is only found in God, and making marriage the end goal has resulted in disappointment and disillusionment for many, many couples who hoped marriage would be just the "fix" they needed. That's not a slight on marriage, because marriage was definitely His idea—but when we place our hopes in *anything* other than God it will ultimately be unfulfilling. If you think that sounds like an overstatement, look at what the Old Testament prophet Jeremiah says. God tells Jeremiah to stand in front of the Temple and prophesy that the nation of Judah will face judgment and punishment if the people don't change their ways.

> Do not trust in deceptive words and say, "This is the temple of the LORD, the temple of the LORD, the temple of the LORD!" If you really change your ways and your actions and deal with each other justly, if you do not oppress the foreigner, the fatherless or the widow and do not shed innocent blood in this place, and if you do not follow other gods to your own harm, then I will let you live in this place, in the land I gave your ancestors for ever and ever. (Jeremiah 7:4–7)

Without some context, it can be easy for us to miss what was happening in this passage. The people of Judah were under the impression that they were automatically "right with God" because the Temple was located in their capital city of Jerusalem. But God reminds them several verses later that Shiloh in Israel had been the location of the Tabernacle[3] for many years, yet Israel had still faced consequences for disobedience. In other words, God is cautioning His people that it can be easy to get so focused on something *that is important and highly valuable* to the degree that they miss out on being in relationship with Him, which is the ultimate goal. In many ways, the Temple had become kind of a "lucky rabbit's foot" for the people; they thought as long as they had the Temple, they were set up for success. It's obviously not a perfect analogy, but I believe we sometimes use marriage in a similar attempt to reassure ourselves that we're doing the right thing and we don't have any changes to make. In other words, we sometimes use marriage to "hide" from God. Not in the sense that being married is easy and never challenges us to grow, but in the same way that God's people in the Old Testament pointed to the Tabernacle and the Temple as the sign that all was right for them. When we point to marriage as a marker of our success and maturity, we miss the point. I (Dan) like to say that we're in love with the word "marriage" rather

---

[3] The Tabernacle was a mobile precursor to the Temple during the years of wandering in the wilderness and the early years of Israel being established in the Promised Land. It was moved to Shiloh in Israel (Joshua 18:1) when the land was divided up between the tribes and remained there during the time of the judges.

than the true journey of growth, surrender, and maturity that fully engaging in a deep relationship with our partner will ultimately produce.

The truth is that we're not created specifically for marriage, but you might get that idea from the way some people talk about it. We're created *with* purpose, *on* purpose, *for* purpose—as male and female to holistically reflect the image of God, the One who made us. God gives us different and unique ways to reflect the kind of relationship that He has with the rest of the Godhead and invites us to experience with Him and with each other. One of those is marriage. But that is all under the umbrella of our surrendered life, not giving into sexual desires and temptations for our own temporary pleasure. We were created for the purpose of living in alignment with God's calling on our lives. If we're married, we live it out in our marriage and also in the rest of our lives. If we're single, we live it out in our singleness and also in the rest of our lives.

In *The Deeply Formed Life*, Pastor Rich Villodas shares the text of an email from an unmarried counselor who attends their church:

> For so many, singleness is the visible sign (stigma) of being "not chosen." It carries the pain of feeling unloved and unlovable, undesired and undesirable, lonely and alone. For many, it means a life lived in limbo, postponing or despairing of living a full life "until" marriage. I believe those are lies from the pit

of hell, because they "steal, kill, and destroy" (see John 10:10), and Jesus came to give us abundant life marked by righteousness, peace, and joy in the Holy Spirit.[4]

After reading those words, you can see there are some people around you who are feeling left out by the way Christians often talk about marriage. It's not done intentionally, but it's still causing pain. We would be well served by remembering that Jesus wasn't married. Neither was the Apostle Paul. If we establish marriage as *the* goal, we have to acknowledge that the central figure of the New Testament (Jesus) and the central author of the New Testament (Paul) both fell short of it. We can't really hang on to marriage as the be-all, end-all if we are faithfully reading the New Testament. In other words, making marriage the ultimate goal is clearly missing the point!

Again, the goal here is not to devalue marriage in any way, but to bring it into proper perspective. Marriage reflects the type of relationship and connection that God desires with us. It's a temporary picture that helps us to see we're called to a better (and eternal) version of connection with God. Recently, a client told me (Brad) that he'll never get married because he experiences same-sex attraction. People have told him, "That's too bad. You won't experience the fullness of who God is without ever getting married." If that statement were true, it would make marriage

---

[4] Rich Villodas, *The Deeply Formed Life* (Colorado Springs: WaterBrook, 2020), 158.

the *only way* we could truly experience or know God. That makes marriage our salvation, which it clearly isn't. And isn't meant to be.

For parents, it's key to let your kids know it's healthy to pursue marriage if that's where they feel God is calling them. *But they need to know it's even better and more in alignment with what God created us for to find our peace, fulfillment, and hope in relationship with Him.* That means we change our language from "when you get married" to "whether God calls you to a life of marriage or a life of singleness" in order to better express the fact that the highest goal for a meaningful life is not marriage itself, or singleness itself. The ultimate purpose and goal of our lives is to pursue God.

And *that* is the difference between people who are living a life devoted to Christ and those who aren't. If Jesus is the Lord of our lives and if we aim to be Kingdom citizens, that means we follow and submit to the ways of the King. For people who aren't aiming to be citizens of the Kingdom of Heaven, they have the option to choose to live with themselves as the ruler and final decider of what is right and wrong. And in that world, it really is an anything-goes approach to sexuality. Because the individual can set themselves up as the ultimate authority and decide that doing exactly what they want to do must be okay and right. That doesn't make it true, but we all have the choice to live like it's true. Think back to the moment of the Fall. The serpent convinces Adam and Eve that they have the option to be "like God." He offers them the chance to set their own course and to *finally* be in charge. But what actually happens is a catastrophic break in their relationship with the Creator, as well as banishment from Paradise and the assurance that producing and sustaining life will be hard work (Genesis 3:16–24). Trying to set ourselves up as the ruler and ultimate moral authority in our own lives today has similarly disastrous results.

In sharp contrast to Adam and Eve's effort to rule their own lives (not to mention our own efforts to do the same), Jesus the true King lived a life of suffering; a life of obedience rather than pursuing His own wants, needs, and desires. Ours is a King who has modeled surrender and dying to self in every last way. Not because He was a masochist, but because He knew that God's design was bigger and fuller than what anybody had previously imagined. And it was bigger and fuller than what we can accomplish on our own by pursuing our own hopes and goals.

But even with Jesus's life as a model, we still find ourselves wanting to be the ones in charge. We have a natural desire to impress upon Scripture our own God-likeness and our own ability to make the rules and decide what is right and wrong. But that doesn't work. In fact, when we reach this impasse, it means that something has to change. We either have to change Scripture to fit what we want to do, or we have to surrender and be changed as a result. Where our logic and our desires are out of alignment with Scripture, it's not Scripture that needs to change; it's our logic and our desires. And to be completely honest, that feels deeply unfair to us.

But when we lose sight of the Kingdom, we can miss the point. We can start to think that the ultimate achievement in life is to be in full control of everything. We all know the feeling of desperately wanting control, of wanting to determine what's best for us on our own terms. Sometimes parenting can feed into our worst impulses in that respect, because we do have the ability to determine for ourselves and for our kids what is best—especially when our kids are small.

But we must continually remind ourselves how likely we are to come to even that conversation with our own wants and desires and will. If we do, we will pass that unsubmitted attitude along to our kids (maybe without even realizing we're doing it). It's key to submit every aspect of the guidance we give our kids to God and to approach it in light of His Kingdom. Ask yourself how much you're imposing your own guidelines and rules compared to how much you're teaching them about God's expectations. If we never take the time to examine that, we may not even realize that we're encouraging our kids in *our* direction rather than God's. What we believe will ultimately end up guiding our behavior. Not what we *say* we believe, but what we *actually* believe.

The Talk

If you plan to wait until your kids ask you about sex to talk to them about it, then you need a new plan. Just know that by the time they're asking, it's already too late for you to get the first words in. Bringing it up yourself *will not* result in your kids pursuing porn or sex or masturbation, and waiting as long as possible to have these conversations because it's uncomfortable for you all but guarantees they will get faulty and not-God-centered information from someone else. But if you talk with them about this in the context of what the Bible says, your kids will have the chance to see their bodies the way God does rather than through the lens of what the world is communicating about them.

I (Brad) once asked my nine-year-old son if he has ever had an erection. We talked about this in the context of him getting older and growing up. He didn't laugh or get uncomfortable about it because I wasn't making a joke about it, and I didn't approach it like an awkward conversation. We had a normal chat about the fact that this would happen from time to time, and I explained that he'll one day have a wet dream. As adults, we know this is just as much a reality of growing up as the fact that puberty brings body hair for all, voice changes for boys, and menstruation for girls. To avoid talking to our kids about these things does them a disservice. Even if we're struggling because we associate these changes with their soon-to-be-budding sex drives, skipping out on the conversation doesn't delay the inevitable—it only leaves our kids in the dark and confused as they experience these changes.

Think about this for a moment: Jesus had a penis. He was a flesh-and-blood man who had the option of giving Himself pleasure. But because He lived a perfect life, He consistently chose to say "no" to temptation and lust in this way. In other words, speaking to our kids about their genitals is not and *cannot* be a bad or wrong thing. They're just part of the human body. Moving from male to female genitalia, it's important to understand that *the only reason* the clitoris exists is for sexual pleasure. I'm not saying this to be edgy or controversial; I'm saying it because it's important that, as parents, we understand that genitals are part of our kids' bodies, and helping them learn about them is like helping them learn about their eyes or ears.

It's interesting to see the light go on in people's minds when they first hear this, but it's important to remember that the awkwardness around this conversation isn't from *your kids* feeling shame about it. They don't know. The awkwardness around this conversation comes from you. We talk with our kids freely about their eyes or elbows, but then we whisper when we talk about a penis or vagina because we carry shame around sexuality and gender as topics. Instead of making them off limits, it's important to figure out how to normalize these conversations in our home.

The sad truth is that a lot of us grew up demonizing curiosity. We thought curiosity about sexuality was sinful in and of itself. And because curiosity was off limits (or at least felt like it was), we haven't created healthy spaces to have these conversations about things that are good and beautiful. When there's no safe place to have these conversations, the taboo curiosities can only be explored secretively. But if you have an open conversation with your kids, it will go a long way toward helping them talk through their questions with you rather than trying to figure things out on their own, or with friends or even strangers online.

It's really important for this to be an ongoing conversation that we never view as being "done," and that we never limit it merely to physical expressions of sexuality. If we stop there and only talk about the physical, fleshly pleasure, we're definitely missing something. We're minimizing what God intends. When we dig into it, we realize that a sexual connection points to a deeper (and truer) point about a spiritual reality: There is a deeper and more meaningful connection with God available to us than we can imagine. When you see physical or sexual pleasure being sought at the expense of connection, that's an opportunity to remind your kids what God is like and what He's created them for.

CHAPTER 5

GENDER AND SEXUALITY

Dan Seaborn and Coach Brad Klaver

In this chapter, I (Dan) am mostly going to pass things on to Brad Klaver, who leads our coaching division at Winning At Home and works regularly with individuals and families on gender and sexuality-related topics.

But before I hand things over to him, I want to set your expectations. This chapter has a lot of information, and much of it may be new to you. For me, reading through it feels like drinking from a firehose! So this chapter will probably be one you will need to take your time with; perhaps you read it in sections or re-read it a couple of times. You will see as you get into it that this chapter is not about making a point; it's about how to lead with love around the topics of gender and sexuality.

Brad's Story

I (Brad) have personal experience with same-sex attraction. My wife Michelle and I have been married for nearly thirteen years and have four kids—but if I had grown up in a world like today's, I may have been pushed in a very different direction and be living a very different life than the one I have today. So when I write about how to have this conversation with your kids, I speak as somebody who has been on this journey and walked it with many, many individuals and families. I'm a certified Christian leadership coach, and in that role I see individuals, couples, and families who are navigating the highly nuanced waters of sexuality, sexual orientation, and other topics surrounding the lesbian, gay, bisexual, transgender, and queer (LGBTQ) conversation.

As you can imagine, my experience with same-sex attraction has pushed me to ask a lot of questions and to work through a lot of struggles that weren't addressed in the church settings where I grew up or spent my young adulthood. I often felt loneliness, shame, and exclusion based on the way people talked about sexuality and identity in faith settings.

It's important to know that, even though I'm married, I still experience same-sex attraction. But just like anyone else with a sexual orientation (i.e., everyone), the goal is not to overcome or change it, but to steward and surrender it to Jesus. For years, the daily invitation from God has been and will continue to be, "Will you trust Me with your sexuality?" And that's the same invitation He gives to each of us—no matter our sexual orientation. When I choose to trust Him with it, I experience His goodness, redemption, care, and fulfillment in ways I have needed it most—in ways I could never experience it fulfilled in any earthly way.

So in this chapter, I will focus on living in the tension between holding to biblical beliefs and standards while maintaining relationship with your kids who may be wondering about their sexuality or gender identity. While we will clearly discuss what Scripture teaches, as Dan mentioned earlier, the goal of this chapter is not to "prove a point." Instead, we want to help parents lead this conversation with love, because the truth is that a lot of people are losing their relationship with their kids over these issues.

Last chapter's explanation of a Christian sexual ethic didn't specifically address how that ties in with sexual orientation or identity, but this chapter will, because Scripture does talk about the connection between husband and wife in a meaningful way. Genesis 2:24 describes that connection by saying "a man leaves his father and mother and is united to his wife, and they become one flesh." Paul later quotes this verse in Ephesians 5:31.

The Genesis passage containing this idea comes after God created Eve and described her in Hebrew as *ezer kenegdo*. Those two words are translated as "a helper suitable for him" in the

NIV. But different interpreters translate these two Hebrew words in many ways. Here are some of those translations to give you an idea of the variety:

"a helper who is just right for him" (NLT)

"a helper fit for him" (ESV)

"an help meet for him" (KJV)

"a helper [one who balances him—a counterpart who is] suitable and complementary for him" (AMP)

Unger's Bible Dictionary gets at the depth of meaning with "a help as his counterpart."[1] The way most of us have seen that passage over time gives the idea that Eve was there to help Adam, but many of the translations over the years have left out the idea of Eve being a counterpart. In light of the fullness of the meaning of this phrase, we see that the biblical idea here is that Adam and Eve are "the same, but different." That idea is key to understanding God's intention for sex and sexuality. Often, the argument for same-sex relationships or sexual activity is, "As long as it's monogamous and committed, then it's okay." But the reality is that when God set up sexuality and marriage, it wasn't just about human pairing and personal fulfillment, but one expression of His much bigger desire for connection and relationship with all of humanity. In other words, God is always reaching out to His creation and seeking connection.

You see both that desire for connection and the "same, but different" language in the way God pursues His people.

---

[1] "Helpmeet," *Unger's Bible Dictionary* (Chicago: Moody Press, 1957), 468.

Throughout Scripture, He calls us His "children," or His "sons and daughters" (e.g., Luke 6:35, John 1:12, Romans 8:16, 2 Corinthians 6:18). This indicates "same" in that we're part of the family, but "different" in that God is the parent who is responsible for the children. The male-female partnership of marriage is also one of the ways God expresses this idea in Scripture. In Ephesians 5:22–33, Paul uses the picture of a husband and wife to describe the relationship between Christ and His Church. That helps us see that God formed us to be connected to Him and in relationship with Him in a very intimate way.

We as the "dearly loved" are called to open up to Christ and His presence. There's a similarity between sex itself and the intimacy Scripture is talking about: in a sexual encounter, the woman "opens" herself to the man, who "enters" her. It's obviously an act of physical intimacy, but there's also something happening on a much deeper level than that: the physical act also creates a connection in the soul and spirit; we become fully connected to our partner, and that is a picture of the kind of connection God seeks to have with us.

When we miss that point, we miss out on what God is calling people to. Just as males and females are the same (human) but different in that we have interlocking parts that connect in sexual expression to potentially create new life, we share a sameness with God in that we're created in His image and because we can connect with Him, spirit to Spirit. We also are able to bring life to the world around us. That is why God considers sex to be a

sacred thing between humans; His design for sex is within marriage, the covenantal relationship between one man and one
woman for life.[2]

Nowhere in the Bible will you find a passage that affirms
same-sex sexuality. We believe that is partly because the idea of
sexuality is a deeper metaphor that teaches us about the connection between God and people. Therefore, same-sex relationships
will always inherently miss that key point, and as a result, they
fall short of His design for sexual expression.

It's important to have a scriptural basis for understanding
God's good picture of sex and sexuality. That understanding will
be key for us as we journey with somebody who is asking questions about sexuality or gender, or even somebody who is telling
us they are sure about their sexuality (and it falls outside of a
biblical standard). Understandably, these are challenging conversations to have with our own children; we find ourselves needing
to figure out how to balance being loving and generous people
while also communicating that God's desire for His people is to
only express ourselves sexually within a marriage relationship.

How to Approach the Conversation

The parents I (Brad) often interact with find themselves
suddenly having to talk with their kids about sexuality or

---

[2] To dig deeper into the intersection of faith, theology, sex, and sexuality, we
recommend *Our Bodies Tell God's Story* by Christopher West.

gender identity because their kids are pushing for the conversation. Our kids are constantly surrounded by this issue in our culture. They may already have begun exploring their own gender or sexuality, or even have come out as gay, lesbian, bisexual, etc. (As you probably know, the phrase for somebody acknowledging their non-straight sexuality or non-cisgender[3] identity is "coming out.")

I'm finding that a lot of parents want to have a single conversation in which they attempt to fully express their thoughts, and then think of this topic as "covered." But the fact that our culture wants to regularly have this conversation with our children forces parents to do so as well. Trying to have the full talk in one shot wouldn't work any better than trying to teach them how to read in an afternoon or how to drive a car in an hour. It takes time and repetition. This will be an ongoing process of showing up, listening with curiosity, and speaking truth in love.

First things first: how you respond matters. Regardless of what the initial conversation with your kids looks like, it's important to do everything in your power to remain calm and keep your own emotions out of it as much as possible. That's obviously incredibly hard, but the way you react and the things you say in this moment can have a lasting impact on your child—for better or for worse. And, just as you are, they're navigating this without much of a road map. So even if you're terrified, angry, or ashamed,

---

[3] "Cisgender" is the term for people whose biological sex matches the one they identify with.

do your best to keep a level head and be gracious as you listen to them discuss their emotions and experiences.

For parents whose child has not just come out to you, it's important to realize that you have the luxury of choosing how to respond if this conversation does come up at some point. You only get one chance at a first reaction. If this were to happen in your family, what would you want yours to be? Do you want to have a chance to get to know your kids as they truly are? Their sexuality is not their core identity, but it's absolutely a big part of it. If you're open and approach the conversation with curiosity in order to better understand their experience, you can meet them right where they are.

Knowing that the way you respond to your kids is often colored by your own experiences, it's important to deal with the reality of your own brokenness surrounding sexuality and to separate that from what your child is dealing with. Digging deep into your own stories will be very helpful in talking about sexuality with your kids. When we experience God's grace, forgiveness, and love toward us in our own brokenness, shame, and curiosity, it leads to healthy and less-awkward conversations with our kids. Remember that it's not about having one "absolutely correct" conversation about sexuality; it's about having an open and ongoing conversation that makes room for curiosity and free discussion, with the ultimate goal of pointing toward God's best and what He's calling your child to.

We need to let our kids know that curiosity is okay and no topic is off limits—but that doesn't mean no *behavior* is off limits. In order to have this no-boundaries conversation well, we must do some healing of our own. We may be afraid of sex and not see it as a beautiful gift from God. We may worry that discussing it will push our kids toward it or will scar or scandalize them. But the truth is that avoiding these conversations doesn't make the curiosity go away. Not having this conversation doesn't mean that your kids won't learn about these things. Instead, they'll take their curiosity and questions to friends at school or church, to the internet or music or movies, or they'll find a friend who is equally curious and they'll explore things together.

Often, the questions that our kids ask may point to a deeper conversation they want to have with us. For example, your teenage son may bring up the topic of masturbation. If your response is only, "No, we don't do that. That's not something that we do!" it may leave him feeling like his curiosity has been shut down in favor of a black-and-white rule. If, instead, you respond to these types of questions with curiosity and work to figure out what is going on with your kids, it can lead to a bigger conversation about sexuality and pleasure. If you ask about their experiences, you will have the chance to help them see healthy ways to be curious about their body, and it will make them much more likely to come to you with other questions later on.

If you're looking for a script for this conversation, you're going to be disappointed—not because we don't want to help, but because you *can't* have a script for talking with a unique and complicated human being about something this complex and nuanced any more than you could have one for teaching your kids to be kind and empathetic. If you're telling your kids something that you don't believe yourself, that you haven't experienced, or that you're uncomfortable discussing, they are likely to notice.

As awkward and intimidating as it is to have these open and honest conversations with our kids, it's absolutely better than the alternative. If we are unwilling to discuss these issues, we're essentially saying, "I trust that somebody else will parent my kids better." I'm sure that's not what any of us think or want, but there's no such thing as "not making a choice" in this situation. If we're not addressing the topic because we'd rather avoid awkward, challenging moments, or because we're afraid of saying the wrong things, we're leaving that conversation hanging out there for somebody else to have with our kids. And they *will* have it.

One of the ways to get to a healthy spot within yourself so that you'll be able to have this conversation is to have open and regular discussions with somebody else in your life about sexuality and gender. This could be your spouse, counselor, coach, pastor, or friend. Something that is often repeated in many Twelve-Step Recovery Programs is "We're only as sick as our secrets." From a Christian perspective, we think that sin goes one level deeper than that, but addressing our secrets is an absolutely huge first step that Christians sometimes (or often) skip!

Regularly engage with God's heart for you around the topic of sexuality. We all have that brokenness. And when we're faced with our own brokenness, our initial defense mechanism is to say that our brokenness isn't as bad as some other kinds of brokenness.

That seems to be at the core of many Christians' response to people with sexual orientations and gender identities that are different from our own. Just like we call stealing "more sinful" than lust or lying (because we're likely to do those two things, but pretty unlikely to steal something from a store), we call non-straight expressions of sexuality "more sinful" than "minor" things like porn use, casual heterosexual sex outside of marriage, and lustful thoughts. We do this because it's human nature to create "others" and to be able to define the ways in which we're better than they are. It seems to help us combat our anxiety around our own brokenness. The word *seems* was chosen intentionally in that last sentence. It doesn't *actually* help relieve any of our guilt and shame. But we're somehow convinced that it will.

But the more we dig into our own experience, the more we realize that trying to "measure" brokenness is not an effective approach. Falling short of God's standard is falling short, and all of us do it! It doesn't play out the same way for each person, and some expressions of brokenness lead to more severe consequences. We all experience brokenness differently. But as we each allow God to meet us in our own brokenness, we'll be in the position for grace and love to overflow as we pass those truths along to our kids.

This goes a long way toward helping to create an environment in which you can speak with your kids about their experiences of sexuality and gender with loving curiosity and truth rather than shame. The bottom line is this: Keep showing up to have the conversations.

Gender and Sexuality as Identity?

When we normalize the conversation about sex as a whole, it naturally feeds into being able to have the bigger conversation about nuances. And sexuality is such an identity marker today that we can't afford to wait to have these conversations. In other words, kids who are searching for a place where they belong can find full and complete acceptance in groups that are based on their sexuality rather than on their interests or skillset. Think about it for a minute: the reason that the categories of "jocks," "nerds," "band kids," etc. exist is because kids in middle school and high school need to find somewhere that they belong. For generations and generations, kids have found "their place" in the previous categories or by joining the robotics team, the artistic crowd, the stoners, or any other number of groups. If you don't think that group identity is a big deal, just imagine how you feel when you see somebody with a shirt or bumper sticker supporting your favorite sports team's rival, or the political candidate who ran or is running against the person you support. Group identity matters, and it runs deep. And now kids and teens (and adults) have the opportunity to find their identity by being part of a movement that embraces a variety of sexual expressions.

As broken people, we will all find ourselves drawn to align ourselves with something that is not our ultimate identity. Our own brokenness leads us to want to find our value and identity in things that aren't going to fulfill us. But it's important to understand that your child's version of broken sexuality is no more broken than your own. *Anything* that draws our attention away from finding fulfillment in God is brokenness. Your inclinations to be attracted to things that artificially fulfill you aren't better or worse than your kids' inclinations. Whatever draws us away from fulfillment in God takes our focus away from truth and goodness. And when we lose our "True North" in that way, we pursue what we're genuinely longing for in other places. In other words, attraction to anything that we think will fulfill us and give us rest apart from God is broken. When we make money or success our goal, it's missing the mark just as much as if we were expecting our sexual partner to bring us that fulfillment that only God can provide.

What Do You Want?

I (Brad) coach individuals, parents, and families through issues of same-sex attraction, gender dysphoria, and several other sexuality and gender-identity issues. Time and again, I see parents who are feeling frustration, disappointment, and fear at the thought of not being able to have grandkids or not being able to tell their church friends about their kid's new boyfriend or girlfriend because they already know how they'll react. Or they're worried that God will no longer love their kids. If you're experiencing those thoughts right now, it's important to know that those are very heavy—and very real—fears.

When I talk with parents, I ask, "What do you want me to do?" Their typical response is that they want me to help their kids realize that they're not actually gay or lesbian or bisexual—just confused. Often, parents view this as the goal because then their fears would subside. My response is always something along these lines: "So you want me to make your kid be straight? I can't do that. I can't actually figure that out for myself." (If that sentence seems off to you, it may be helpful to understand that there is a difference between attraction and actually acting on attraction. I can't force myself to only be attracted to the opposite gender, and I can't help my clients experience that either.) Instead, I talk about the importance of surrender—which means bringing our thoughts and actions in line with God and His standards. That's not just for kids; that's also for each of us as parents. The goal isn't a changed sexual orientation, but a deeper orientation toward Jesus.

(Go back and read that last sentence again, because it probably wasn't what you expected me to say. And you may have disagreed with it when you first read it.)

Instead of being "solution-focused," here's what I encourage parents to do: Listen far longer than you think you need to listen. Ask open-ended questions. And when you ask questions, make sure the purpose is to understand what this journey has been like for your child. Chances are, if your kids are coming out to you, they haven't been thinking about it merely for days. They've probably been thinking about this for quite some time—maybe even years. They've either been working through it on their own—which is incredibly lonely—or with their peers, which isn't always the most helpful thing.

In today's culture there is a high demand for kids to come out as something other than straight immediately and to make that their identity. As we discussed earlier, just as adults do, they seek group identity to feel secure and to find belonging. In his book *Understanding Sexual Identity*, author Mark Yarhouse makes the distinction between "Big G Gay" and "little g gay" to talk about the difference between identity and experience. When kids come out, it often means that they found the ability to relate to the experience and connected with it, but then they jump right to identity and belonging from that point.

If your kids are younger, you may already be familiar with this story: JoJo Siwa is a dancer and YouTube influencer whose fan base is mostly upper elementary and lower middle school-aged kids. She came out on an Instagram video, but she wasn't very specific about things. She said she was part of the LGBTQ community, but didn't really describe or define what she meant by that. For the next fifteen minutes, the comments section of her stream was filled with people celebrating with her as she talked about it. What kid isn't looking for that kind of affirmation? What adult doesn't want that?

When I ask my clients what being gay or trans causes them to feel, they often give an answer that addresses a deficit in their core longing to belong. In John 1:38 (NRSV), Jesus asks two disciples who are following Him, "What are you looking for?" That wording resonates deeply, because we're always looking for something. If each of us examines our inner motivations when we make decisions, we're likely to realize that we're looking for connection, affirmation, and desire.

When those pursuits take us in healthy directions, we celebrate that. But when those pursuits go in negative directions, we can be filled with shame and demonize the misstep. There's nothing wrong with feeling guilty or bad about unhealthy choices, but it's important to realize that going that route often causes us to miss the reality that what we are actually seeking is good. So if your kids are finding identity in their sexuality or gender identity, they're looking to get their core needs of identity met—but that's a need only God can meet. In other words, they're seeking it in the wrong place. But the seeking *itself* is a good thing!

The goal here is to see how this process can happen. Kids will have an experience and feel a certain way about life based on that experience. But lots of kids who've come into my office saying they're trans realize after more conversation that they don't feel like they fit into the masculinity their dad models, or they don't feel like a girly girl. That's different.

It may be helpful for parents to remember that when we're talking about kids who are ten, eleven, or twelve years old, they may not even fully understand what sex between two people is. (When I [Brad] first understood that I was attracted to other boys, I wasn't thinking about having sex with other boys. I didn't understand that at all.) Talking with kids who are young will be very different from conversations with adult kids who are coming out to you. It's easy to get ahead of ourselves and start assuming very young kids are planning out their whole lives, but they often are just trying to figure out how to navigate what they're feeling and how to live based on that.

Your kid sharing his or her experience with you does not necessarily mean he or she is going to be in a same-sex marriage. It doesn't automatically mean that he or she wants to have same-sex sexual encounters or gender-reassignment surgery. It might just mean that his or her experience of the world doesn't map cleanly on what issues like these are "supposed" to feel like, and he or she is now trying to make sense of it.

Regardless of how these conversations start or where they go, it's important to remember that for Christian parents, the highest goal isn't to get our kids to be straight or to move them from being trans to identifying as their binary gender. As parents, *our highest goal is to help point our kids to Christ.* When we follow the King, our lives will reflect Him, and our goal will be to glorify Him. And when we draw near to Jesus, we can't help but be transformed by Him.

Sexuality, Gender Identity, and Mental Health

It's important to know that the mental health disruptions young people (and adults) who don't experience life as cisgender or heterosexual face are, unfortunately, very real. This makes sense if we put ourselves in the shoes of those who feel socially isolated or alienated from many of the people around them.

Often, the clear communication kids receive is that anybody who isn't cisgendered or opposite-sex-attracted is "other." Maybe you've seen the pro-inclusivity bumper sticker that says, "Be careful who you hate. It could be someone you love." That's not to say that you should start ignoring the biblical sexual ethic we've talked about, but you don't have to affirm same-sex relationships or people transitioning genders in order to realize that there is a difference between believing that our faith gives us a guideline for sexual behaviors and communicating (explicitly or not) that people who are attracted differently than you expect or who identify differently than you expect are people to fear, shun, or hate.

In fact, Jesus's opponents thought they were making a devastating critique when they called him a "friend of sinners" (Matthew 11:19), but we know that wasn't an accident. Jesus went to the places of pain and brokenness instead of choosing to only spend time with people who were part of His "group." Chuck Colson said it well when he described what it looks like to follow Jesus in our love for others:

> Isn't it interesting that Jesus didn't set up an office in the Temple and wait for people to come to Him for counseling? Instead, He went to them—to the homes of the most notorious sinners, to the places where He would most likely encounter the handicapped and sick, the needy, the outcasts of society.[4]

The idea of belonging (or not belonging) is key in understanding why the rates of depression and suicide (and suicide attempts) are higher among LGBTQ youth than they are among the general population. When people feel (and often are) excluded, they retreat. They often seek solace not in community, but in isolation and in coping behaviors. This isn't just

---

[4] Charles Colson, *Loving God* (Grand Rapids, MI: Zondervan, 1996), 200.

true for same-sex-attracted or gender-nonconforming young people. Think about your own responses to stress, frustration, and disappointment. Your go-to coping mechanism is probably some kind of unhealthy behavior. Whether that's gambling, overeating, promiscuity, pornography use, self-medicating, anger, engaging in reckless behavior, or any number of other things. In addition to unhealthy coping mechanisms, young people often have a hard time picturing how their world might improve. For a fourteen-year-old who feels alone and isolated because they realize their sexual orientation or gender experience doesn't match the expectations of the people around them, there aren't many great options. They can "tough it out," run away, numb the pain, hide, or act out. And if they believe that the next four years (or more) of their lives will be exactly the same, they aren't likely to experience great mental health.

If you've already had some version of a conversation about sexuality or gender identity with your kids and it went poorly, here are a few things that you can do to try to re-engage:

Approach the conversation with grace and gentleness.

Acknowledge that the last conversation didn't go the way you'd hoped—not because your child didn't fully agree with your perspective, but because it didn't end up benefitting your relationship. Do your best to remember that maintaining the relationship matters most of all. Don't lose sight of that and expect that you will reach full agreement, or you'll see the relationship take a lot of damage.

Remember that this is a process, not a one-time conversation.

It will feel like a lot is riding on the outcome of this conversation, and that is true. But it's truer in terms of the bigger conversation that will take place over days, weeks, and years. Don't get too hung up on how one single part of this conversation goes; remember that the goal is to share your heart, but also to listen to your child as they share their story and their heart.

Be curious.

Not curious in the sense that you're observing something foreign or strange to you, but curious about what your child's personal experiences and thought process looks like. Ask him or her questions and spend time truly listening, not just waiting for your chance to respond and to prove him or her wrong! Your kids need to know that you love them *no matter what!* That doesn't mean you have to abandon your beliefs—it means you're remembering that love and openness will get you further than condemnation and harshness will.

Remember these things:

- This is new turf for you, too. You won't do it correctly at times. It's a journey together, so make sure you focus on the fact that you love and care for each other.
- You can control your own words and responses, and your child will choose theirs. Spend your focus

and effort on being solid and secure in the things
you know to be true.

- Notice and accept things about yourself through
this journey. Remember that you are imperfect, and
see this as an opportunity to grow in the skills
required to be an effective parent.
- Don't be afraid to seek wise counsel for yourself
and your child. It can be very helpful to have a third
party involved to help each of you see some things
about the other person's point of view that you may
be missing on your own.

These conversations with your kids will be tough, but do
your best to prioritize your relationship with them over full
agreement. This topic will be very emotionally charged for everybody involved, so you'll all have to work especially hard to avoid
saying things you will regret later and that you won't be able to
un-say. Approaching these difficult topics with love and grace is
especially important!

Frequently Asked Questions

Can my child experience same-sex attraction or come out as LGBTQ and still be a Christian?

Yes. Salvation is through Christ alone. Our becoming or
being a Christian is not dependent upon our own good behavior

or rule-following (praise the Lord!), but upon the shed blood of Jesus. A person's experienced sexuality, orientation, or gender identity is not a disqualifier of the work of Christ in their lives. Rather, it is an area of life that one must continue to bring into the light, surrender to God, and invite His loving truth to have the last word over, just as with every other area of life where our desires conflict with His. As we addressed in the chapter, attraction is different than behavior—just as it is for those of us who are attracted to people of the opposite gender. Just as each of us has to navigate (and surrender to God) our lustful desires or our attraction to people other than our spouses, so your child's sexuality, orientation, or gender is something he or she will need to continue to surrender to His lordship. In fact, those very things, surrendered under the loving care of God, can actually be a pathway to greater intimacy with Him.

My child never previously showed signs of being anything other than straight or cisgendered. Could it just be a phase that he or she will grow out of eventually?

Many times, this idea comes from a parent's perspective that "all kids experiment" in some way, shape, or form, and will at some point "straighten up." At other times, parents are so filled with fears or anxieties about the future that they label it as a "phase" as a coping mechanism. While sometimes it is "simply a phase," that is quite often not the case. More often, your child didn't choose his or her sexual orientation or attraction any more than you chose yours. So, to approach this with a "phase" perspective will often keep you from engaging in this conversation with the type of intentional, heart-level, and ongoing connection your child needs. If you believe this is simply a phase to grow out of, you may be tempted to believe that if you ignore the issue, it will eventually go away. This can be incredibly hurtful, confusing, and damaging to your child. Once again, your child's sexuality or gender is not a problem to be fixed or a phase to grow out of; rather, it is a very specific quality to be stewarded, discipled, and loved, regardless of how uncomfortable the process might make you.

Is experiencing same-sex attraction a sin?

The short answer is "no." To expand, simply experiencing same-sex attraction (or being gay in sexual orientation) is no more or less sinful than being straight. Our attractions or orientations don't make us sinful or holy—rather, it's what we do with our attractions and orientation that counts in the eyes of God. Attraction is not the same thing as behavior. While same-sex sexual behavior is clearly not permissible according to Scripture, a person experiencing same-sex attraction or orientation does not automatically mean he or she will take part in same-sex sexual behavior any more than a person who experiences opposite-sex attraction or orientation will automatically take part in heterosexual sexual behavior. For this reason, if we say, "Being gay is a sin" and move on, we risk condemning people for their unchosen orientation toward the same sex, falsely communicating that people must become straight in order to follow Jesus.

How should I respond if or when my child comes out or is asking questions about his or her sexuality or gender?

There are several keys to keep in mind here.

- Stay calm: Your first response is the most memorable one.
- Aim for connection.
- Build safety for ongoing conversation.
- Curiosity is key: Ask about your child's experience, how this has impacted him or her, or what it has been like. This will address his or her core need of being seen, known, and understood.

How can I best walk with my child through their journey of sexuality and gender over the long run?

- Pray and think: What is God's goal for my child?
- Ask questions to understand their experience, not to confirm your assumptions.
- Listen longer than what is comfortable.
- Ask for forgiveness. Perhaps you have said things in passing about LGBTQ people in the past, or maybe your response to your child was less than loving. If so, God gives us the ability to acknowledge our mistakes, ask for forgiveness, and repair the relationship.

- Stay connected to your child's heart. Remember that he or she is a person to be loved, not a problem to be fixed.

CHAPTER 6

DEVELOPING AN APPRECIATION FOR SCRIPTURE

Dan Seaborn and Pastor Steve Norman

All Christian parents want to create a home environment where their kids learn about and appreciate Scripture, but many struggle to actually do it. There are plenty of factors that make it hard: families are so busy that there isn't much time to be intentional about taking time to focus on Scripture; the messages from our world and culture drown out the truth of God's Word; and it's hard to find organic teaching moments that connect more than superficially. If you've been running into one of these barriers, or others not listed here, this chapter will give you some practical ways to help your kids engage with Scripture.

Steve Norman will be joining me in addressing this topic. Steve and I have both served as pastors for multiple decades, and we both have four kids—so we've each spent time working to tackle this problem head-on and will share some of the practical ways we've engaged with Scripture in our homes. But first, we want to share a few "big picture" principles that guide how we engage with God's Word.

Basic Principles

As parents, we can only give away what we have.

We're going to start strong right out of the gate with a challenge to every parent reading this: If you want your kids to embrace, value, and digest Scripture, you have to set that example. You need to make spending time in the Bible a priority in your personal faith journey and in your marriage. The reality is that having your kids in church once a week or sending them to a Christian school is not a replacement for your personal relationship with God being lived out under your own roof. What your kids see, hear, and experience at home will be what they consider "normal," so be sure to set a good example with your own reading of the Bible and applying it to your life.

Additionally, think about all the other things you've taught your kids over the years. You taught them how to talk, dress themselves, feed themselves, ride a bike, and swim. You taught them how to behave in public and how to share toys with friends and siblings. What all those things have in common is that *you were teaching them a skill you already had yourself.* You couldn't teach your kids to talk until you knew how to talk. You can't teach your kids how to shave time off their 50-meter butterfly if you don't know how to do anything fancier than a dog paddle. In the same way, you have to be in the Word if you want to be able to teach your kids biblical truths. If you want your kids to value Scripture, you have to set the example by being ahead of them on the spiritual journey. You need to help lead and guide them as they grow, learn, and struggle.

For every parent reading this, we'd like to encourage you to take a moment to think about your own practice of reading, meditating on, and memorizing Scripture. Before you can apply it to your life, you have to know what the Bible says. As you read this chapter about how to help your kids develop an appreciation for Scripture, we're challenging you to first evaluate your own. When you run into a dilemma, how many other sources do you seek out for advice before you turn to God or read His Word? When you're confronted with the fact that your behavior is out of alignment with God's standard, how do you react? Do you get defensive, minimize, or deflect? Or do you choose to submit and surrender, even when it's hard and frustrating? None of us does this the right way all the time, but if you want your kids to grow in this area, you absolutely have to lead by example!

Scripture must be seen as dynamic and life-giving.

The Bible is God's Living Word; it's not a formula or a math problem. In other words, while God's truth is unchanging, we will hear what it is saying with fresh ears at different seasons in life. The Bible is not at all similar to a novel or a textbook that you can read one time and absorb all the useful or important information. If you're having a hard time wrapping your head around this idea, think about how different verses about anxiety or mourning seem to jump off the page at you when you're going through a tough time in life. Helping your kids learn this will have a huge impact on their understanding of when, why, and how to read the Bible.

If they think of it as just another list of rules rather than a way to actively hear from God, your kids won't view the Bible as something to turn to when life is tough. They may actually start to view it like Job's friends did while he was going through incredibly difficult times in life: as a way to explain *why* Job was facing such difficulties. But because Job's relationship with God was personal—not just a religious intellectual understanding—He helped Job see that His Word reminds us that *He is with us* even in our difficulties!

Scripture should inform our family lives in moments of discernment.

This almost goes without saying, but life is confusing. And the Word of God is a gift in moments where we need clarity. The Bible speaks specifically to many situations we may find ourselves in—and when we can find that direction, it definitely makes it easier to know the way forward.

But there are also lots of circumstances we will face that don't have a clear-cut answer in the Bible—and that's actually one of the reasons continually engaging with Scripture is so valuable. It gives us perspective on God's character. The more we know what God is like and what He cares about, the easier it will be for us to use that information to make decisions when it's hard to know what we should do. Books like Proverbs, Ecclesiastes, and Paul's letters inform how we can navigate confusing moments in life.

Scripture should inform our family lives in times of crisis.

The Gospels, the Old Testament prophets, and Psalms are a huge gift to the people of God in times of trial. They remind us of the call of God as well as the reality of suffering. All of Scripture speaks to this, but these specific books really focus on God's faithfulness and the Holy Spirit's ability to empower us when we're stuck.

When it's time to make tough decisions, our first response is often to depend on some of our deepest and most natural habits. That will usually mean we try to control as much of the situation as possible. When control and a quick fix are our goals, it's tempting to put our faith to the side until we've dealt with the crisis. But if we can stay disciplined and avoid that initial impulse, we can set a better example for our kids to see as we instead choose to make these decisions through the lens of our faith and by taking God's Word seriously.

Scripture reflection should be both meals and snacks.

Sometimes it's good to have a verse to think about in the car, or a line that younger kids can sing. But it's also important to make sure we're hearing and appreciating passages of Scripture in context. Based on where our kids are in their developmental stages, we can pursue unique approaches to biblical engagement.

People generally fall into two categories when it comes to discipline. Some are good about taking a day-by-day, consistent approach to things like eating well and exercising. Others are much more all-or-nothing and try to "make up" for less healthy decisions with sweeping changes or extreme, short-term diet or exercise binges. What we're advocating here is that you don't approach reading your Bible that way. Instead, use a combined approach in which you consistently engage with Scripture, and also dig deeper sometimes as a family.

God meets us in Scripture through our highs and our lows.

There is a temptation for Christians to pretend life is always great. Think of the phrase "I'm too blessed to be stressed." When we hear those kinds of ideas over and over, it can make us think there's something wrong with us if we're discouraged, angry, sad, or worn out. We think we are supposed to paste a smile on our faces and be ready to tell anybody who asks that we're doing great. But what we see in Scripture is a willingness to discuss the highs and lows of life. We see Jesus mourning and experiencing agony. He mourned the death of His friend Lazarus before He raised him from the dead (John 11:33–36). He wept as He looked out over the city of Jerusalem and wished the people would repent and turn to God (Luke 19:41–44). In the Garden of Gethsemane, He agonized over His coming crucifixion to the point that He sweat drops of blood (Luke 22:41–44). The fact that Jesus Himself experienced these deep negative emotions should show us that negative emotions *in and of themselves* are normal and healthy to feel. The issue we run into is that we often overreact when we feel a negative emotion, and we do or say something that we end up regretting. That definitely should be addressed, but it's important to understand that Scripture has multitudes of references to people (and God!) experiencing negative emotions. In other words, the emotions themselves aren't inappropriate, but our unhealthy responses are.

The Practical Ways We Engage with the Bible

With those principles as a guide for the way our families engage with Scripture, here are some of the practical ways that Jane and I (Dan) made it "normal" to talk about the Bible and faith in our home:

In addition to having our kids involved in youth group and church on Sundays, we did a couple of key things on a regular basis. We found a great teaching tool that gave short, kid-level versions of Bible stories. The cards we used were small and had an illustration on the front and the story and a few questions on the back. (The exact tool you may use isn't the key; the important thing is to find some way to make God's Word a regular part of family life.) When our kids were very young, I would read one story, which would take maybe two minutes, after dinner. Then I would read the questions and have the kids answer them. The first few were about the facts of what we'd just read—who the main characters were and what they did. But the last question was always intended to create discussion. It focused on what these stories told us about God and about how He wants us to live.

As the kids got older, the answers to that last question became more impactful. I think closing out dinners with a short, kid-friendly Bible story went a long way toward making it normal and common for us to talk about spiritual things as a family. And because we had those conversations on a near-daily basis at the end of a meal, I think it also made the kids more open to sharing about their spiritual lives throughout the rest of the day. Again, the important thing isn't that you find a tool just like the one we used, but that you find some way to create an environment where you regularly touch on and talk about spiritual things.

Another thing we did required more effort and greater sacrifice. I've always been drawn to the arts. It's not unusual to hear me break out in song at home or in my office, and when the kids were young, I put that tendency to good use: I started by putting a couple of Bible verses that I wanted to help them memorize to music. I didn't write a song or add actual music to anything; I just added a little rhythm to the verses and sang them. Jane and I started singing these verses with the kids each night as we were tucking them in at the end of the day. After they memorized the first few, I added another. By the time we stopped tucking our kids in, there were about fifteen to twenty songs in the collection. And I'm a pretty energetic guy, so it wasn't long before some of the songs had motions and involved jumping around on the bed.

That's where the sacrifice came in. Obviously, by that point in the day, Jane and I were looking forward to some kid-free time, and nighttime routines are generally geared toward bringing the kids' energy levels down. But we wanted to make sure ours enjoyed this time as a family and that these verses got deeply embedded into their minds. So we opted to make that sacrifice and bring their energy level way up right as we ended the day.

I'm not saying you need to do either of those things, but those are some of the practical things we did to make the Bible a regular part of our lives and our conversations as our kids were growing up. I won't lie, it would have been easier not to do them. But if we hadn't been intentional about them, we easily could have gone a week (or longer) without having a Bible-based conversation.

As important as it is to use the Bible as a template for your household rules, it can be tempting to do so in a way that actually kind of turns God into the "bad cop" and you into the "good cop" who isn't making the rules, but merely enforcing them. This approach might prevent your kids from getting frustrated with you in the moment, but it is much more likely to create a lifelong disdain for faith or God's standards and expectations. If God is mostly invoked as the judgmental disciplinarian, think of how much resentment a child might store up against Him. Even when you work hard to stress His loving and forgiving nature, if all your kids experience are the rules, they're likely to develop some issues.

Many of us who grew up in religious homes probably had this experience ourselves. Our parents may have used God as a kind of "elf on the shelf" or Santa Claus to remind kids that He's always watching and "He knows if you've been bad or good." In other words, parents knew there would be lots of time each day when they wouldn't be able to directly supervise their kids, so they made sure to remind them that God was always watching. Even though that's true, this statement typically feels more like a threat than anything else. Kids frequently hear this reminder/warning in a way that makes them think God is waiting for them to make a mistake so He can swoop in and punish or judge them. And not only is He waiting for it, He's probably excited about doling it out.

As Christians, our goal is to help our kids to draw closer to God, so we need to make sure we're doing our best not to make God into a judgmental observer rather than a loving Father who wants to be in relationship with His children. Balancing love and justice is a nuanced idea that's hard to explain to kids (and hard for us to understand ourselves). Because, of course, God does care about our thoughts, words, and actions lining up with His standards. Eugene Peterson clarified the distinction this way: "In Scripture, God's anger is always evidence of God's concern, his involvement, his commitment to his people."[1] But Jesus tells us the story of the Prodigal Son, which adds a softer angle to God's love. The beautiful part is that even though the son has burned all his bridges and wasted all his father's gifts to him, the father still runs out to greet him and to welcome him back home. When we teach our kids what God is like, we need to make sure we're giving that balanced perspective, because we've all heard the often-repeated joke from people who walked away from faith (or never had faith to begin with) about God "striking someone down" or lighting them on fire if they tried to walk through the doorway of a church. Those jokes aren't funny, and it's hard to tell if they're even meant to be. They seem more like coping mechanisms from people who see God as an angry version of Zeus or Jupiter—not the Father who wants to give good gifts to His children.

It's important that our desire to help our kids learn and follow God's standards for their lives doesn't come at the expense of their desire for a relationship with Him. Clearly, some kids will just naturally and innately rebel against any rules that are put into place; that's not what we're talking about here. We're cautioning you not to let the *rules* part get in the way of the *relationship*. That's definitely a fine line to walk in determining when to respond with forgiveness and grace and when to respond with punishments and restrictions— but it's important to find a way to walk that fine line. It

---

[1] Eugene Peterson, *As Kingfishers Catch Fire* (Colorado Springs: WaterBrook, 2017), 32.

probably looks different for different families, and even for individual kids within the same family. That alone can cause some conflict and frustration.

If you're exasperated by trying to figure out how to walk that line, that's normal. But while you're working through that, remember that Jesus forgave sins (Matthew 9:2; Luke 7:48) and also told people to go and sin no more (John 5:14; 8:11). He didn't always take a hard line, but He also didn't always back down and move on quickly. We're not Jesus, so we shouldn't be surprised when we mishandle things from time to time as we try to do the right thing for our kids. But it's important to take inspiration from Jesus and not use Scripture as a "battering ram" in our home when we want to put our foot down or get the last word. There's a difference between choosing to be faithful to what God calls us to and ruling by the letter of the law.

If you are more of a black-and-white thinker, this will probably be especially hard for you. In my own marriage, I (Dan) am the rule-breaker and Jane is the rule-follower. Our parenting has benefitted from these different approaches to life (though it has also caused plenty of tension and conflict), because it has helped balance each of these tendencies out. I help Jane see that not every rule is equally important, and she helps me see that rules help make sense of the world—and that's especially true for people who are wired a certain way. Just as we discussed previously, no single approach will be effective. Whether you make life "all rules" or "no rules," you will leave your kids with serious deficits in their understanding of God and life.

When They Go Elsewhere for Guidance

When kids and teens have adults other than their parents in their lives who can offer spiritual guidance and encouragement, that's wonderful. But this section is going to focus on what to do when they're seeking guidance from people who are not trying to point them to God, and may even be pointing them away from Him. Your kids will inevitably look to people they shouldn't for guidance and direction. If your child's personality skews toward being more conscientious, this might just be a speed bump in his life's path. He may get some outside guidance and quickly realize he feels guilty or doesn't like the consequences of his choices. If your kids are more curious, risk-taking, or rebellious, then this stage may last quite a bit longer.

Whether they're straying a lot or a little from biblical teaching, your primary role as a parent is to be there for them, no matter what. That doesn't necessarily mean clearing things up so they never face consequences, but it also doesn't necessarily mean punishing them to the fullest extent when they mess up. I (Dan) wrote a lot about the experience of having a wayward child in the book *Parenting with Grace and Truth*. Jane and I have lived through it, and the absolute last thing I want a parent with a wayward child to get out of this chapter is the idea that I have a solution for them, or that if they had just done things differently, they wouldn't be experiencing this. Those things aren't true. If you're in that spot, know that my heart hurts for you and I know what you're going through. Keep doing what you can to turn your hurt and fear and anger over to God.

Whether your kids are straying off the path a little bit or a whole lot, there will be times when they seek out friends, significant others, or even online communities for guidance and get some bad advice. As a parent who loves them deeply and wants the best for them, it really hurts when they do that. I know it can feel like they're sending you the message that you didn't teach them the truth, or that you didn't have their best interests at heart. But do your best to avoid believing that you've figured out what is going on in their heads, because the reality probably has more to do with them feeling left out or feeling like they're missing something other kids are experiencing.

God's Word calls us to lives of discipline and surrender. As adults, we know how hard that can be and that it means saying "No" to some things we think would probably feel good to say "Yes" to! Your kids feel the same way, and they might be looking for input from other people because they know their guidance will be much more likely to allow for (or encourage) indulgence in things God tells us to avoid than yours would be. If that happens, it doesn't mean your kid is bad or that he's intentionally denying God. It might just mean he is awash in hormones and making decisions based on feelings or impulses rather than on what he's been taught.

If each of us considers our own lives, there are probably some areas where we are resistant to what God wants for us as well. We may be holding on to some habits we know God wants us to surrender. Or we may be avoiding spending time in prayer or reading certain passages of Scripture because we know God will use those moments to convict us of something we know we shouldn't be doing. For some reason, it's easy for us to miss seeing these things in our own lives, while it's pretty easy to see when our kids are doing it. This isn't an excuse for us to stop being obedient and faithful, or for our kids to act that way. It's simply a reminder that knowing and having access to the truth doesn't guarantee changed behavior.

I (Dan) have written about this idea before, but it bears repeating here: As parents, we often blame ourselves when our kids make mistakes and don't stay faithful to the things we've taught them. But when we read the Creation story in Genesis, we don't get to the point of the Fall and then blame God for the choices Adam and Eve made! That story powerfully (and painfully) reminds us that people have the capacity to make unwise and unhealthy choices. Adam and Eve did. We do. And our kids will, too. When it happens, it can be easy to feel like a failure as a parent. But that's not fair, and it's not a true reflection of reality. Your job as a parent is not to continue making choices for your kids as they grow up and become adults. Your job is to teach them the truth, to model what it looks like to love God and His Word, and to be there for them as they work to live it out.

As they become adults and maybe have families of their own, some kids will hold on to what you taught them and retain their love of Scripture. Others may not. Just remember that you don't call God a failure based on Adam and Eve's decisions, so don't call yourself a failure as a parent based on your own children's decisions. In fact, if your kids are walking away from the faith they were raised in, the best thing you can do is stay faithful and continue to model a life that is shaped by a love for God's Word. That means you live a life of surrender, grace, compassion, confession, love, forgiveness, and peace.

As I will discuss further in Chapter 10 ("I Love You No Matter What"), the key thing in disagreement is to keep the relationship intact. I know that it is very, very painful when your kids (and maybe grandkids) aren't pursuing a relationship with God, but no amount of begging or berating them is going to change that. Instead, devote your passion and energy to calling out to God and asking Him to work in their lives. We all know we don't have the ability to change people, but God does!

I want you to remember that parenting is a matter of broken people raising broken people. We will never do it perfectly. Our tendency as parents is to try as hard as we can, and when we fail, we often feel very defeated. The more we learn to do our best and continually point our children to God and His Word, the better off we will be. Our kids may fully reject all things having to do with God—but that's where we have to remember that our responsibility is to teach them the truth and leave the rest up to Him. They are His kids first—we simply have to carry out our responsibility well. In the end, we will answer for what we did, not what they choose to do. We live to honor God and trust the outcome to Him.

CHAPTER 7

IT TAKES A TEAM

Dan Seaborn and Pastor Steve Norman

You've heard the phrase "it takes a village to raise a child." That's the idea my wife and I relied on as our kids were growing up. As you see from the title of the chapter, I'm updating the phrasing for the twenty-first century. Like all parents throughout history, Jane and I knew we were largely unprepared and had no idea what to expect in many different situations. We wanted to have a "team" in place to support us and to share their wisdom and experiences with parenting, so we came up with a way to involve people we respected as we raised our kids.

We did that in two ways. First, we created Our Team. We got support and insight from other parents while our kids were still very young. We talked with them about their rules and the things they prioritized as they were raising their kids. And second, we worked to partner with other adults who would be positive role models for our kids as they got older so that they would have Their Team. Both parents and kids need support and help from teammates along the way!

Our Team

The system didn't work perfectly, but I believe Jane and I used a lot of wisdom when we chose our teammates. The parents we relied on for advice helped us make sure that Jane and I stayed on the same page and worked together to accomplish good things for our kids.

I was a youth pastor and family life pastor for ten years, so I had the benefit of watching lots of kids grow up before we ever got past the "childhood" stage with our own children. As I watched teen after teen finish high school and launch into adulthood, I learned that vastly different parenting approaches all seemed to result in mature and well-adjusted teenagers. The converse of that was true as well: vastly different parenting approaches also seemed to result in immature teenagers who struggled to adjust and who struggled with discipline and making good decisions.

Over the years, I saw that kids can grow up in very strict homes and turn out great—or not so great. That was true of very lenient homes as well. I found that this was not the essential piece of the puzzle for raising children well.

That surprised me, and it may surprise you as you're reading this. Growing up, I was always taught being stricter with your kids is best for your family. My own home life wasn't great, so I always suspected that wasn't entirely true—and over the years, I have discovered that some beautiful things can come from thinking differently from many of the people around you. Though that can be stretching and straining at times, it can be very productive in raising your children to have a biblical perspective on life and to be prepared for the world coming their way.

When our oldest kids were small, I started paying close attention to parenting styles. Both strict and lenient parents ended up with some great kids, so we knew there had to be more to the story than we had initially assumed. To find out more about what those parents were doing to succeed, Jane and I identified three couples who we admired for raising mature and well-adjusted teens and young adults and we took them out for dinner and talked with them about what they valued as parents.

We wanted their insights because we saw that their kids were growing up to love the Lord; they were mature and in a good place. To get a variety of perspectives, we chose one couple who had firm rules and standards, one that had very few rules for their kids, and one that was somewhere in the middle. Surprisingly, all three had common threads, such as the importance of treating people kindly, the importance of faith, and the importance of the parents setting the standards for the household.

We didn't just take those threads and use them as our new family rules. Afterward, Jane and I spent time praying and listening to God about what the rules and expectations would look like in our home. We ended up with five things we called "Mom and Dad's Rules of the Home." We printed and framed them. Although all our kids are grown and out of the house, we still have the original copy. The design is dated and it's obvious that we created the file in a word processing program twenty-plus years ago. But while the design and layout are very much relics of the past, the rules themselves still hold up.

I'm not going to share those rules with you here. If I did, you'd be tempted to try to replicate what Jane and I used. But I am encouraging you to look at parents of kids about ten to fifteen years older than yours whom you admire. Talk with those parents and work on putting together your own list! If you're a single parent, this can be particularly beneficial: You're facing trials and tribulations that many people won't ever face, or even understand. It will also be helpful for you to get perspectives from other adults, some of whom might be wired more like your kids than you are!

If you like this idea but are struggling to think of what you would ask, here are a few questions to help you start:

- What do you wish you had handled differently?
- Which of your rules are you most glad you prioritized?
- Did you have any rules that you eventually abandoned because you no longer saw much value in them?

- What do we need to prepare ourselves for that you didn't see coming? What caught you most off guard?
- Did you have some rules that worked perfectly with one of your kids but failed spectacularly with another?
- When you didn't agree on an approach, how did parenting strain your marriage? How did you handle it?

Now, I want to offer a few disclaimers and cautions. First of all, there is no "formula" that will guarantee your kids grow up to follow the path you hope they will. Your job is to teach them truth and the right values and morals. But just like everyone else, our kids have the ability to make their own choices. We all hope and pray that they will grow up to love and serve the Lord, but there is no step-by-step way to ensure that happens.

Parenting isn't as simple as making rules and sitting back as you watch your children and teens joyfully follow them. Kids are very good at testing boundaries and can be absolutely dogged in working to find out *exactly* where the line is that you won't allow them to cross. Just know that even if you come up with the perfect set of rules (which I don't think actually exists), you will still run into issues. I mention that only because I don't want you to discard your rules a few months into the process because you feel like they're not working!

Ultimately, *making* rules is a whole different deal than *enforcing* rules. If you're having a hard time implementing rules in your home, I would strongly encourage you to seek out a counselor who works with children or adolescents. Many counselors work exclusively with families who are going through these types of growing pains, and it's helpful to know you're not alone and that bumps in the road don't mean you're doing something "wrong."

The second disclaimer I want to share is about the couples whose wisdom and advice you are seeking. You might find a parent or two who will try to do more than just advise you and share their own approach. If you feel like you're moving from getting advice to the point where somebody is trying to control you, it's perfectly fine (and healthy!) to walk away. Parenting your kids is ultimately your responsibility, and if somebody tries to walk all over you and take charge, it's important to remember that. It's great to get help, but if people are crossing the line, it's fine to ask them to respect your boundaries and give you some space.

Their Team

You also need to establish that same sort of team around your children. They are growing up with lots of voices speaking into their lives. I'm not just talking about music, videos, or advertisements, but also influencers, other online gamers, and people they don't even know who are commenting on their posts or videos. That's before we even talk about their friends, classmates, teammates, or anybody else they interact with over the course of a normal day. It's not that all these interactions are threatening, because most of them will be harmless or neutral. But some of them will leave your kids with a skewed understanding of what is "normal" behavior or thinking. Look back to your own childhood and teen years. You probably enjoyed watching people cross the line a bit, even if you were more of a rule-follower yourself. Those small, subtle interactions can slowly define reality and goals for your children, which is why it's so important to make sure they're getting (at least) an equal amount of positive, uplifting, and godly input.

One of the ways to do this is to look for people both you and your child admire and ask them to be involved in your child's life. The only real limit to who this could be is your imagination. Maybe it's a family friend, a principal, or a pastor. Or it could be a coach or a volunteer at your church's youth group.

Make sure to pick people who will be invested in your kids' lives, because there will be days when your kids don't want to speak to you. If your kids are young right now and you can't picture that, you'll just have to trust me. Like any close relationship, there are times when conflict and disagreement are so strong that everybody just needs some space to talk things through with somebody else. That's just part of normal family life. When those days come, it's critical to have another adult they feel comfortable with, who invests in them, and with whom they can have a conversation.

Also, think about how many times your spouse or somebody else you're really close to tells you something about yourself that you don't want to hear. It can be easy to dismiss their thoughts. (I'm not sure why that's the case, but it happens for all of us.) But when we hear that same thing from somebody else, it hits us in a different way and something "clicks."

I'm sure those of us who are married have gone back to our spouse and said, "Guess what I figured out today?" And when we tell them, they say, "Yeah, I told you that a few months ago and you ignored me." It happens all the time. And it will happen with our kids too: They'll hear the same advice or instruction we've been giving them from somebody else and immediately accept it. When that happens, it can be tempting to get into a big conversation about why they ignored us when we said it, but do your best to ignore that impulse and just take the win!

For our children, these strategic relationships and conversations with other adults were foundational in making sure they stayed true to some of the biblical values and truths that were important in our family. Hearing a similar message from another adult always seemed to help them realize that Jane and I weren't as off base as they initially suspected. In moments when we had disagreements or different perspectives, having a third party for our kids to bounce ideas off was extremely helpful.

Leveraging Grandparents

My (Steve's) parents have been open with me about some of the mistakes they made as they raised me and my siblings, and one of the things they are committed to as grandparents is constant improvement in those areas. That's not specific to my family, either. For many grandparents, grandchildren are a chance to revisit some of the issues, themes, or practices they may have missed with their own children. This doesn't mean they approach it as a "do-over" or a way to undo past mistakes, but the arrival of grandchildren gives people who've raised their own kids an opportunity to reflect on both the "wins" and "misses" they had with them—and to come alongside their adult children with new humility and wisdom.

The story of Eli in the book of 1 Samuel is a great example of this. Eli was the high priest who served faithfully for many years. When he grew older, his two sons took over his role. But they weren't faithful in their service to God. Instead, they used their elevated status to look out for themselves and to take care of their own needs and desires. First Samuel 2:12 says it like this: "Eli's sons were scoundrels; they had no regard for the LORD." Just to remind you again: the parent is not fully and forever responsible for their children's behavior, adult or otherwise. But it does seem fair to say that Eli's parenting had probably not been the greatest, considering that *both* of his sons were corrupt and used their office to manipulate and dominate people.

But the thing Eli is most well-known for is not his relationship with his sons. Many people recognize his name through the story of Samuel.

Samuel was dedicated to God's service at an early age by his mother. He grew up serving at the Tabernacle and learning under Eli's tutelage. One night, Samuel heard a voice calling him; he kept going to Eli and asking him what he needed. But Eli hadn't called him, so he kept sending him back to bed. The third time Samuel went to him, Eli realized that God was speaking to him and told Samuel: "Go and lie down, and if he calls you, say, 'Speak, LORD, for your servant is listening.'" Samuel followed that guidance and as a result, he became the prophet God used to lead his people for many years. He anointed the first two kings of Israel, one of whom was King David. While he wasn't technically Samuel's grandparent, Eli definitely functioned in that role, and he clearly took the time and effort to correct some of the inattentiveness that had been present as he raised his own two sons.

If you can relate to the story of your parent making some mistakes with you but now wanting to be very involved in your children's lives, hopefully this Old Testament story encourages you. Even if you're still working through recovering from some of the wounds your parents caused as you were growing up, it's important not to overreact and put boundaries in place that are too extreme. But it's also important not to put your kids in danger just because people with a history of being abusive happen to be biologically related to them. If abuse was part of your past, please seek clinical and godly counsel as you figure out how to allow (or not allow) grandparents to be involved with your children.

For those who didn't deal with abuse but had other hurts and disappointments as you were growing up: if your parents want to take an active role in the lives of your children, that's great! Invite it. And know that, even though they said and did some hurtful things that have stayed with you well into adulthood, they most likely want to correct those behaviors as they interact with their grandkids.

My (Dan's) parents had a unique opportunity to do that with my youngest daughter. Jane and I grew up in North Carolina and South Carolina, respectively, and raised our family in Michigan after I took a job as a pastor there. Unfortunately, that meant our kids got to know their grandparents mainly through annual trips down south to visit both sides of the family. It was definitely hard on us to know they wouldn't get to know their grandparents the same way they would have if they had grown up near them.

But, at the same time, we were both happy to put some distance between ourselves and our childhoods. I'm going to share some of the difficulties of mine here—not to trash my parents or to get you to feel bad for me, but because I know some of you are reading this and thinking, *I could never expose my kids to what I went through.*

My dad was abusive and controlling. Jane's had walked out on the family when she was a kid and she saw him once a year or so. Both our moms had picked up as much of the slack as they could, but Jane's mom was an overwhelmed single parent with six kids living in poverty. My mom was a sweet, faithful, kind woman, but my father controlled her, too. I won't go into detail, but my childhood was marred by abuse and lots of ugliness.

When our youngest daughter went through a rebellious phase in her mid- to late teens, we were at a loss. We wanted to get her away from the people she was spending time with, but we didn't have the option of moving away. So we sent her to live with my parents in South Carolina.

I was constantly surprised to see how the parents I had known as strict disciplinarians who were completely inflexible and very judgmental embraced Anna during this wild phase. She didn't move down there and become a completely different person, but my parents showered her with love and affection instead of judgment and punishment—*not* how they raised me. Anna got to know a completely different man than the father I had grown up with. I don't know if he mellowed out simply through the passing of time or if he was intentionally allowing God to mold him. Still to this day, I'm stunned, to be honest—because Anna thinks of Grandpa as this sweet, mild-mannered guy who was always there for her and who was willing to do anything to help her. My experience growing up couldn't have been more opposite. I won't lie: there's a part of me that envies the relationship Anna had with my dad—but I'm beyond grateful that she got to have it!

I know some of you reading these words have had a wide variety of experiences with your parents. Your childhood might have been filled with abuse and torment, or it might have been idyllic. To think we can trust every grandparent to invest in our kids is just not realistic. I'm completely against putting your kids into a situation where they are likely to experience the physical, sexual, or emotional abuse you may have received at your parents' hands, but I'm also against writing them off as lost causes when they may have truly changed and deeply want the opportunity to make a positive impact in their grandkids' lives. If you're walking a difficult line there, I would encourage you (again!) to reach out to a counselor—both to work through anything that you still need to process from your own childhood and to explore what it would look like to involve your parents in your kids' lives.

Grandparents as Historians

One of the side effects of people becoming so geographically disconnected from our families is that we lose a lot of our family history. Some of you reading this may have grown up near your grandparents, and some of you didn't. As I (Dan) mentioned, my kids didn't grow up around theirs, and when they were still living at home, Skype, FaceTime, and Zoom were much less prevalent than they are now—in fact, for my older kids, those tools were completely nonexistent for a while. But now, distance doesn't have to be a limiting factor in involving grandparents as part of the "team" that invests in your kids! Of course, a mostly virtual relationship will be different and will certainly make quality time together a lot more difficult to come by, but it's a big upgrade over trying to stay in touch via sporadic phone calls or mailing letters back and forth.

This idea isn't completely free of complexity. Not everybody has parents they *want* their kids to learn from, and we completely understand that. But please remember that the fact that your parents made mistakes when they were raising you doesn't mean they're lost causes. Even if you don't see eye-to-eye on several big life issues, their ability to connect your family's present and future to the past is hugely valuable: they can share stories of great-grandparents, and maybe even further back. But more importantly than serving as family historians, they can serve as faith historians. My (Steve's) parents were children of the Great Depression. They have stories about God's provision and faithfulness from a completely different era. These stories of God showing up in our family's history have been a gift to my children—serving as a reminder that God can be trusted, even in the most trying circumstances.

We see this many times throughout Scripture. Moses and Samuel often talked about the importance of the Israelites teaching their children and their children's children about what God had done. In 2 Timothy 1:5, Paul mentions Timothy's grandmother Lois by name as he is encouraging and reminding Timothy of his family's legacy of faith. Grandparents aren't just able to offer wisdom because they've been through similar situations and may have learned some lessons the hard way; if they are followers of Jesus, they can also share how they learned to depend on God, how they went through ups and downs, and how God was faithful all along the way.

Again, there is no "formula" to guarantee that your children grow up to love and follow God, but having grandparents who can pass along a legacy of faith can have a huge impact on your kids. In addition to hearing it from you, it is so important that your kids hear these truths from adults other than you, and many grandparents have acted in that capacity for generations. If you're fortunate enough to be able to give your kids access to the stories, experiences, and wisdom their grandparents have gained over a lifetime, please make sure to do so!

We sincerely hope that you spend some time in prayer and listen to God as you work to actively engage other godly adults as part of the team that will help shape and influence your children as they grow up. Understand that this approach works for two-parent families who live next door to their children's grandparents, and it also works for single-parent families who live a thousand miles away from any of their relatives. The key isn't even how long you've known the adults who will make up your child-raising team; it is that they are people who are genuinely seeking after God and committed to coming alongside both you and your kids—people who will encourage and challenge you along the way.

Putting these teams in place will take prayer, time, and energy, but it's worth it. If you already feel overwhelmed with everything you're juggling right now, you may be tempted to skip developing these relationships. But please take the time, because they will truly benefit you and your kids more than you might think!

CHAPTER 8

HELPING PARENTS PROMOTE AND MODEL GOOD INTERPERSONAL SKILLS AND BOUNDARIES

Dan Seaborn and Dr. Emilie DeYoung

Kids and teens today have many different options when it comes to communication. They're used to texting, video chatting, Snapchat, TikTok, Marco Polo, and whatever new apps have been developed in the time since this chapter was written! It's great that they're learning the skills to communicate virtually—but unfortunately, these skills don't often translate to communicating well in person.

Some research suggests that the first four seconds of in-person communication are crucial to making a good impression.[1] In

---

[1] Duane Elmer, *Cross-Cultural Servanthood* (Downers Grove, IL: InterVarsity Press, 2006), 48.

addition, the kids and teens that I (Emilie) meet with share that they feel anxiety and a sense of unfamiliarity when they must have "direct" communication with others, especially adults, over the phone or in person. With that in mind, it's especially important to help our kids learn how to communicate confidently and well in these types of conversations. Unfortunately, adults often react with frustration or ridicule instead of taking the perspective that they can help teach the next generation. In the same way that it takes us time, energy, and practice to keep up with the apps, memes, and lingo our kids use, it will take them time, energy, and practice to learn the things that seem like common sense to people who grew up in a world that is wildly different from today's.

This means we will need to intentionally teach them the importance of things like eye contact, body language, and speaking clearly and at an appropriate volume. It will also include learning that much of the dark, mean-spirited, negative, and inappropriate humor that is seemingly everywhere online is not the right way to talk to people in person (or online, but that's a different conversation covered briefly in the technology chapter).

Knowing that our kids and teens may be learning incomplete or flat-out wrong social skills, it's important for us to *model* good ones. It may help to remember that we are preparing kids for future employment and relationships by helping them learn positive and healthy communication skills. Here are a few of the basics to cover.

Awareness/Caring for Self and Others

In Matthew 22:37–39, when Jesus was asked about the greatest commandment, He said, "Love the Lord your God with all your heart and with all your soul and with all your mind." Then He went on to talk about the second greatest commandment, and He said, "Love your neighbor as yourself." These two ideas are repeated throughout Scripture. Much of the law in the Old Testament focuses on these two things—how to worship, love, and obey God; and how to live in community with other people. Over the centuries, believers have often struggled to walk the line of doing both these things well.

In this section, we'll be focusing on the second greatest commandment and the five words *Love your neighbor as yourself.* Part of this commandment about loving your neighbor is something we can easily miss. Jesus ends the command with this key phrase—*as yourself.* Sometimes we get so focused on making sure we're not being selfish that we actually forget that *we* are also immensely valuable people created in the image of God. It's important to teach our kids that every single person is created in the image of God (Genesis 1:26) and matters deeply to Him. That includes each of us as well. Jesus lets us know that loving ourselves and our neighbor are both important to God.

Once we know that all people are important to God, it changes the way we think of treating them, and it's key that we teach this to our children. Knowing that *all* people are immensely valuable to God reminds us to teach our kids to consider the words they use about themselves and others. Are they choosing words that acknowledge their value? Or are they using judg-mental, self-deprecating, or critical words? (As much as this will hurt to read, if their words fall more into the negative categories, this can be a cue to examine your own patterns of speech to see if they learned some bad habits from listening to you.)

I (Emilie) have a client who was on a soccer team. Every time he missed a goal or had the ball stolen, he would become self-deprecating, saying. "I'm so stupid," or "I'm no good at sports!" In spite of his parents' best efforts, this negative lan-guage became "stuck" on his mental recorder. Working with him in counseling, we worked hard to change this language, recognizing that he is made in God's image—and God doesn't make junk. Mistakes are simply part of the learning process; they do not change who he is.

This is the most important point in this chapter. Once they understand that every person is created in the image of God (even the people who annoy them, and even themselves), our kids will be set up with the most important understanding of navigating relationships. Learning how to communicate and interact are great, valuable tools, but it is essential to start with the understanding of *why* relationships are so important and *why* people have such immense value. In fact, God thought people (you and me) were valuable enough to sacrifice His own Son to restore our relationship with Him! With that as the starting point, the rest is basically learning how to express that value to other people.

Learning Compassion and Empathy

As we acknowledge the value of others, it's natural to begin to have compassion and empathy for them. Although they are used interchangeably on a regular basis, there is a key distinction between compassion and empathy. *Compassion* (synonymous with sympathy) is essentially feeling bad when you see other people experiencing pain or dealing with a difficult or challenging situation and feeling compelled to do something about it. This is an important skill for our kids to learn. We can teach this by noticing when others are struggling and helping our kids stop to think about how that person feels in the moment. Remind them that they can try to help relieve pain when they have the ability to do so. *Empathy* moves a step further. It isn't only about seeing when somebody is facing a difficult situation, but the ability to feel what they are feeling. With compassion or sympathy, you are feeling *for* somebody else. With empathy, you are feeling *with* somebody else. So it's not just about your kids noticing they don't want something like that to happen to them; it's them noticing *how they would feel* if it did.

Teaching your kids to empathize is probably the single biggest way to raise their "emotional intelligence." For a long time, we only measured intelligence through schooling, tests, and equations. But that way of measuring it falls short in so many ways. That's why you've heard of a distinction between "book smarts" and "street smarts," which has more to do with navigating challenging or dangerous situations.

In our experience, achieving harmony and peace in relationships has a lot more to do with *how you relate to people* than *what you know*. You may have heard the idea that people don't care how much you know until they know how much you care. In order to do this, it helps to teach kids and teens how to serve and prioritize other people. Even though it may seem that way at first, this doesn't contradict our first point. When you understand that you are immensely valuable to God, you have nothing to "prove" by jostling for position and competing against other people. Instead, you *know* you're free to love and give, because it doesn't take anything away from you. If we can teach our kids that lesson, as hard as it is to internalize and to pass on, we'll be setting them up to love others well. In God's economy, giving, loving, and sacrificing have the highest value. But it's hard to believe that sometimes. It's easy to get caught up in thinking that life is a zero-sum game and that in order for us to win, somebody else has to lose. If we can't get past this way of thinking in our own lives, it will be nearly impossible to convince our kids that they should live in alignment with God's values of loving and serving others rather than the world's values of competition and dominance.

The Art of Communication

As we've pointed out previously, it's hard to teach something that we ourselves don't know or practice. When it comes to teaching communication, that will be especially true, because our kids will see us practice (or not practice) what we're teaching them throughout the day, every single day. In light of that, these lessons on the importance of communication can refresh all of us as we read through them.

Communication is both verbal and nonverbal. In other words, it's not just the words we choose that communicate our message to the people around us. Our volume, tone, facial expressions, and gestures all communicate as well. If you think back over some of the conflicts you've had in life, it's likely that a lot of the hurt or miscommunication didn't actually have to do with the exact words spoken, but with the defensive or attacking tone, the eye roll, or the physical movements that displayed a clear lack of interest.

Though we know that to be true, when most people think of communication, we still think of words. However, some researchers believe that as much as 93 percent of what is communicated comes through things other than the specific words that are used; Albert Mehrabian's highly regarded work on the communication of emotions suggests that 7 percent is communicated by the words we choose, 38 percent by our voices alone, and 55 percent by body language. There isn't full agreement on that idea, but it certainly helps to open our eyes to the reality that we can easily say the "right" words in the wrong way.

This means we have to ask ourselves some tough questions, such as: *What am I communicating when I interact with my kids? Am I giving them my full attention? Where is my phone when my kids are trying to talk to me?* These might not be the most comfortable questions to read, because the truth is that we're all a lot more distracted than we want to be. There are so many different things competing for our attention, so we tell ourselves that we can multitask and get multiple things done at once. That might work for listening to a podcast while driving or talking on the phone while we clean the house. But even then, we have to hit the fifteen-second rewind button or ask our conversation partner to repeat themselves because our attention shifted to the other thing we were trying to do "in the background."

The same thing will happen with your kids. One great way to model healthy communication for them is to allow for fifteen minutes of your day to be completely focused on your child. During this time, you can model "active listening" as you engage with them. This includes good eye contact, an open posture, and a present and engaged mind. This time of connection should be child-centered. In other words, the child gets to choose the activity and the focus of the conversation. While you're doing this, keep in mind that kids often use the "language" of play to communicate. Instead of using words, they often communicate through behavior and play. That makes it especially important for parents to "tune in" to what their kids are expressing through their behavior and nonverbal communication.

One way I've seen this in action is that one of my clients often slammed her books on the countertop and stormed to her bedroom when she came home from school. For several days, her parents ignored the behavior, since it seemed to cool down after several minutes. Finally, one of them gently followed my client to her room and asked if she was okay. She burst into tears and said her friends had been mistreating her at school, ignoring her during recess, saying mean things, and laughing at her in class. After hearing this, her parent gave her a hug and spent some quality time with her making bracelets (my client's choice). In this way, parents can "speak" the language of their child and help them to feel seen and valued.

Handling Emotions

An often-overlooked step in raising kids is helping them identify emotions. For some parents, that may be because they are so adept at handling their own emotions that it's hard to start from the building blocks. But for others, it may be because they aren't especially skilled at identifying emotions themselves. Regardless of how skilled or unskilled you may feel in this area, remember that it's important to help our kids learn to identify emotions. It takes a great deal of self-awareness to recognize an internal experience and label it with a word. In fact, the English language has almost three thousand different words to describe feelings!

So let's narrow the field. As children are developing in their emotional capabilities, we can teach them that feeling words can fall into four main categories, or "Feeling Families": Glad, Sad, Mad, and Scared.

If you're helping them categorize emotions for the first time, a good way to get started is to go through each of these categories and ask them to share an experience that triggered that type of emotion. Then you can explore what other feeling words fit that experience, such as "excited," "happy," or "joyful." It's important to understand that feelings don't only happen one at a time; several emotions can be experienced at once. Let your kids know that's okay and it's nothing to feel strange about. Feeling multiple things at the same time is normal, even if it is challenging to navigate.

Here is a good starting list of feelings broken down into their Feeling Families:

Glad—content, pleased, playful, cheerful, surprised, relaxed, delighted, silly, peaceful, happy, proud, thankful, excited

Sad—empty, hurt, disappointed, lonely, discouraged, ashamed, hopeless, lost, gloomy, crushed, depressed, withdrawn, unloved

Mad—angry, irritated, grumpy, disgusted, frustrated, furious, enraged, hot, annoyed, jealous, impatient, explosive, violent

Scared—afraid, startled, worried, tense, anxious, concerned, alarmed, frightened, shaken, terrified, threatened, embarrassed, horrified

Other—confused, upset, bored, responsible

Once your child identifies his experience with a feeling word, give him "permission" to feel that emotion. *All* emotions should be welcomed and encouraged. Christians don't always think that way, though. We can sometimes think that welcoming or accepting an emotion will mean we will have to be pulled in whatever direction that emotion demands. But the truth is that Jesus experienced the full breadth of emotions when He was living here on Earth.

Three simple guidelines are useful in defining what healthy emotional expression looks like:

Don't hurt yourself.

Taking out frustration with a self-destructive approach is obviously not a healthy way to express it. There are some obvious destructive behaviors that we immediately think of that fall into this category: some people turn to addictive behaviors in an effort to cope, others turn to substances to numb the pain. It's not always that obvious, though. Punching walls or kicking chairs doesn't just harm things, it also harms the aggressor. Many people have broken hands and toes in their attempts to take their frustrations out on inanimate objects.

Don't hurt others.

When kids are young, this will sometimes take the form of physical violence like hitting, biting, or pulling someone's hair. But as people get older, we get more sophisticated about the way we hurt others. Teens know they aren't supposed to hit people, so they often choose to lash out and hurt others in emotional or relational ways. They may use hurtful or embarrassing words. Or they might make a show of directly defying anybody trying to claim authority. Adults can struggle in the same way, so be gracious with your kids as they're learning to avoid hurting others when they're feeling negative emotions.

Don't hurt stuff.

When kids are feeling big emotions, a physical outburst might seem like it's their only option. In those moments, they may be tempted to throw things, kick things, punch things, or slam things. You get it. Again, we've probably all seen adults do some of these things, and when it's an adult or an older teen, the amount of strength and physical force the person brings can make the situation scary rather than simply uncomfortable or awkward. That's why it's so important to help our kids understand this principle early on in life.

Unfortunately, parents often get stuck telling kids what *not* to do, but it can be easy to forget to teach what they *can* do instead. Let's emphasize the ways our kids can take care of their various emotions. When they are glad, it can be helpful to laugh. When they're sad, it can be helpful to cry or ask for a hug. When they're mad, it can be helpful to take a walk. When they're scared, it can be helpful to take some deep breaths or remind themselves that they can do hard things. Building emotional intelligence in our kids will yield healthy emotion regulation, which will help with healthy communication.

Instead of disciplining or criticizing a child for experiencing a certain emotion, you can celebrate the ability to identify it. But the fact that it's good to identify and experience an emotion doesn't mean it's okay to say or do anything that feels right to them. Once your kids successfully identify and accept an emotion, you can help them identify how to best care for it.

Here are some positive ways to express and care for emotions:

Glad—Celebrate by talking with a friend, praising God, praying, making a list of things you are thankful for.

Sad—Cry, ask for a hug, write in a journal, take a walk, listen to music.

Mad—Breathe deeply, do something active like exercising, slowly count to ten.

Scared—Catch your thoughts and pause, take some deep breaths, pray, imagine a peaceful place.

Conflict Resolution

Conflict resolution will require these emotional skills combined with all the other communication skills covered in this chapter. Conflict is part of any significant relationship. It's possible to avoid conflict if you just keep conversations superficial, but any time opinions or preferences are part of a conversation or a relationship, conflict won't be far behind. Many people will do their best to avoid getting into a debate with people they don't know very well, but that's not because there is no disagreement—it's because the insignificance of the relationship means the stakes are low.

That's an important perspective to remember, because many Christians have been raised with the idea that *conflict itself* is an issue. Paul echoes Psalm 4:4 when he writes in Ephesians 4:26,

"In your anger do not sin." This is a good reminder of the distinction between anger and sin. Conflict, therefore, is not inherently bad; the way we handle it is what can become an issue. In her book *The Art of Conversation*, Judy Apps titles a chapter "Enjoying Disagreement," which is a profound concept in and of itself. In it, she writes: "Understand this important truth: good connection is not the same as agreement. You can disagree without losing connection."[2]

As we all know from personal experience, conflict is something people are typically either too reluctant or too eager to enter. Counselors often refer to these different approaches as passive, assertive, and aggressive. Those who are conflict-averse (or passive) tend to be overly accommodating so they don't "rock the boat." Those who are comfortable with conflict (or aggressive) prefer to err on the side of confronting and addressing things "head on." Neither of those approaches is fully right, and neither is fully wrong. Very few people perfectly walk the line of knowing when it's time for confrontation and when it's time to overlook something because the issue isn't worth addressing. Assertiveness means carefully choosing your spots to be firm, but not too abrasive. Whatever approach you use for conflict resolution will be what feels "normal" to your kids.

Therefore, it will be immensely helpful to model healthy conflict-resolution skills. That means choosing appropriate

---

[2] Judy Apps, *The Art of Conversation* (West Sussex, UK: Capstone, 2014), 198.

times and reasons for confronting other people—which inherently includes not confronting them at inappropriate times or over inappropriately minor issues. It also means the level of frustration and hurt that you bring to the conversation is proportional to what happened. If the hurtful behavior is a first-time offense, do your best to keep that in mind as you are confronting the person. If it's a repeated behavior that's relatively minor, keep that in mind too.

Modeling conflict resolution healthily is the best and most effective way to pass it along to our kids. With that in mind, here are a few key points you can teach them:

Pick your "battles."

There will be times when your kids will be angry even though the situation doesn't warrant it. Other times, their reluctance to confront somebody may outweigh their willingness to stand up for themselves and express a clear boundary. Spending too much time on either of those extremes is not good. If your kids explode over small offenses or passively allow major ones, they are unlikely to be long-term fits for good and healthy friendships, romantic relationships, or workplaces. If you can help them learn to choose their battles wisely, they will have a better idea of what is worth addressing directly and what is worth letting go.

One way that I (Emilie) help young people learn how to decide when a situation is worth addressing or not is by talking about disappointments and hurts as things that fall into the categories of "oh bummer" or a "big deal." An "oh bummer" moment might be something like not being able to go to a friend's house for a play date. But a "big deal" moment would be something life-altering, like moving to a new city.

This can be tricky, because "oh bummer" moments often feel like a big deal, and we don't want to minimize things that might be really important to our kids. For example, you might think getting cut from the soccer team would be an "oh bummer" moment, when in fact for your child, it really might be a "big deal" because of the social implications.

Engage proportionally.

The next step is to help your kids learn the degree to which they should push or be upset about a particular situation. If we've already decided that confrontation is appropriate, it's easy to start thinking "I'm right and they're wrong." Once that switch flips, it can be easy to lose perspective on what level of reaction is appropriate and what is overkill. Help your children and teens learn that the "scorched earth" approach, where they lose their temper and intentionally say hurtful things, is not the way to address an offense (even though it may feel good in the moment).

Give in a little.

It is very uncommon for one party to be completely right and the other completely wrong. Help your kids learn that the goal of conflict resolution is not to rub someone else's face in how wrong they were; it is to figure out what went wrong, address it, and then figure out how to move forward. In fact, in a good conflict, no one actually "wins." The goal is understanding, not winning. But our kids won't just figure that out on their own, because our knee-jerk response as humans is to seek vengeance or retribution when we're upset. We'll need to teach our kids (and re-teach them as often as necessary) that resolving conflict *restores* relationships rather than elevating one party over the other. That means compromising by having everybody involved give a little bit.

Don't ruminate.

One of the ways conflict can inflict long-term damage (to your kids and their relationships with others) is holding on to the hurt and the negative emotion from a specific conflict or argument well beyond the timeframe the situation calls for. Make sure your kids know that negative experiences tend to have an outsized influence on us and on our feelings. We know that one negative comment sticks in our heads much longer than ten positive comments would, but our kids don't know that's normal and just the nature of negativity. Help them see that they don't have to let that frustration and hurt fester or unnecessarily bring past painful experiences into the present.

Some Final Thoughts

We close this chapter by focusing on some skills and tasks that might not initially feel like they fit in a chapter on "interpersonal skills and boundaries," but which are also important as kids build relationships and navigate the world. It's important to teach them how to do things like washing the dishes, pumping gas, doing laundry, mowing the lawn, cleaning the bathroom, shoveling snow, vacuuming the house, changing a tire, and cooking a meal.

Every adult will need these skills at some point in their lives, but they aren't things your children are likely to be motivated to learn on their own. If you can teach them some of these practical skills (and others that we didn't list here), it will definitely help them as they grow up and gain more freedom and responsibility.

At some point in life, everyone realizes they are missing a critical skill—and that's not a good feeling. Part of our responsibility as parents is to set our kids up for success, and that means helping them implement some disciplines and learn how to complete some mundane or unpleasant tasks. They may protest and say that they can learn any necessary skills by watching YouTube videos. While that is likely to be true, it's still preferable to change your first tire with somebody there to help rather than on the side of the road in the cold or the rain, trying to replay a YouTube video on the tiny screen on your phone. The more of these practical and essential skills that you can teach your kids while they're under your roof, the better.

But no matter what you're working to help your kids develop, don't get discouraged if change takes time. It will be a process for your kids to learn to identify and responsibly express their emotions. It will take time for them to figure out how and when to confront somebody in a way that leads to a calm, respectful conversation. It will also take them time to learn some of the life skills they will need in order to function on their own at work. And it's okay. It's normal for growth to involve periods of both progression and regression.

If you start to get frustrated that your kids aren't able to change in a short period of time, remember what it takes for you to make changes in your own life. You've probably gone through a series of stops and starts with some of your own spiritual or emotional growth. You've probably started a new workout plan, diet, or "wake up early" routine and given it up quickly when you experienced a setback. So when your kids are struggling to learn new habits, do your best to give them some grace. Because change takes time, even when they see the value in the changes and are willing to work toward them.

CHAPTER 9

I'M YOUR PARENT FIRST AND FRIEND SECOND

Dan Seaborn and Dr. Peter Newhouse

"I'm Your Parent First and Your Friend Second" could almost be the title of any good parenting book. Far too many parents get sweet-talked or guilt-tripped by their kids into going along with things that are not helpful in the long run. In the short-term, you may be able to avoid some conflict by giving in and letting your kids get away with something every so often, but you'll likely do more damage in the long run if you attempt to be the "cool" parent. Our kids are going to be looking at our words and behaviors through a short-term lens, but it's our job to keep the long-term outcomes in mind. And that means helping our kids understand the importance of rules, disciplines, and healthy habits.

I (Dan) have a unique relationship with this tension. As I mentioned before, I am far more of a "rule breaker" and Jane is far more of a "rule follower." But I also grew up in a home with a strict disciplinarian for a father, so what I saw modeled as "fatherhood" was mostly laying down the law and doling out harsh punishments. You can tell from just that brief description that I often had two perspectives warring within me, particularly in my earliest years of parenting: I was torn between being lax, like I wished my own dad had been, and being strict, like he actually was. I'm sure my kids felt the whiplash at times as I bounced back and forth between those extremes.

As I talked to other parents and watched them deal with their own challenges in this area, I realized I wasn't alone in this struggle. *Most* parents have a hard time with this balancing act. There is always a pull to ignore the rules a little bit (partly because it's easier to let things slide than it is to deal with them) and to be the "good cop." Unfortunately, that will either put our coparent in the position of "bad cop," or it will let our kids know our rules are really more like suggestions—and they are already expert boundary-pushers and loophole-finders. That's just a fact.

Kids look to define boundaries, and then test them. Kids who are very conscientious may look to define the boundaries so they can stay within them, but that type of behavior is the outlier rather than the norm. Most will spend time and energy testing boundaries to see where they're weak—and if they find that different parents have different rules, they will work to exploit them. Again, I don't say this to be anti-kid, but to be realistic about what happens when we have rules that we don't enforce or when coparents (whether married, divorced, or blended) aren't consistently enforcing the same ones. When that happens, kids will play one adult off the other.

When my oldest son, Alan, was sixteen or seventeen, he did this almost to perfection. He and his friends came up with an idea to do something that they shouldn't. Then, realizing they were most likely going to get caught at some point, they figured they needed to get at least one parent to sign off on the plan—but they had to choose carefully. They discussed it and picked the parent the group thought was the most likely to approve the plan: me.

Alan knew that even though I was more flexible than many other parents, I wouldn't give my permission for this particular idea—so, he asked for it in the vaguest possible way. He mentioned a couple of general things about what the group was up to, but without enough detail to explain what was actually going to happen. I told him I trusted his judgment and that he should do what he thought was right. He told me later that his thought process was: "Well, he didn't officially say *no*, so we're good to go!"

When Jane eventually found out about what these boys had done, she was upset with Alan. But when he told her, "Dad said it was okay" (which, as you know from what you just read, was not true), she got mad at *me* even though I hadn't done anything wrong. And that made me mad! So then Jane and I were upstairs in our bedroom, arguing with each other, while Alan was downstairs, pleased that he'd pulled his plan off without a hitch.

Once Jane and I realized what actually happened, it was time for Alan to face the consequences. But he sure did everything he could to keep that from happening. That was obviously a frustrating experience to live through, but it's a good example of what can happen when your kids realize that one parent is more geared toward following the rules than the other parent—or in the case of a breakup or a divorce, than their other set of parents.

Tips for Establishing Rules

Make the expectations clear.

While kids will do their best to "stress test" your rules, you can't skip the step of having rules and of making them clear to all involved. If you have unclear rules, your kids will feel like correction and punishment can come out of nowhere without them even having a chance to realize they made a mistake in the first place. As you can imagine, that will be discouraging for them, and kids will often either develop an overactive sense of responsibility or conscientiousness in an effort to keep from making a mistake, or feel like since even their best isn't good enough, they may as well stop trying. You'll want to avoid pushing your kids into either of these responses. You might think that a conscientious, cautious kid is desirable because they're more likely to follow the rules. The problem is that if unclear rules have made your approval a moving target, their conscientiousness will likely be motivated by anxiety and fear.

Stick to them.

Once the rules are established and the expectations are clear, it's important to apply them consistently. Every parent knows the challenge of holding back laughter while you're watching your toddler do something funny or cute, even though it's not something you want them to keep doing. But when your kids get older, the issue is less about their behavior being funny than the fact that sticking to the rules can feel too tiring, or like you're fighting a losing battle. It can be easy to hear your kids fighting and decide you don't have the energy to deal with it. Or to overhear a conversation between your kids and their friends and decide that you don't want to open the can of worms that would result if you were to get involved. But once you stop paying attention to your rules, your kids will do the same.

Enforce the rules in a similar way as your spouse or their coparent.

Having the energy and willingness to enforce rules is hard enough when you only need to motivate *one* person—yourself. But when you add a spouse to the equation, now you're dealing with two different perspectives and approaches. As I mentioned earlier, my wife and I have different views on rules sometimes, so it was often tempting for me to "selectively enforce" some of the ones I didn't think were a big deal. And that meant there were many times when my kids knew they could do or say something when they were just around me, but that they would get in trouble for if Jane was there. Unfortunately, I unintentionally undermined her authority with my selective enforcement. In those situations, it ended up feeling like the kids could think about "mom's rules" and compare them to "dad's rules" and then decide to follow whichever version were the most advantageous to them at that time.

If you're more like me, do your best to stay aligned with your spouse so you don't invite extra conflict about the very idea of rules themselves! If you're more like my wife, do your best to stay open to re-evaluating some rules your partner doesn't agree with. That doesn't mean your spouse gets the final say every time, but be open to letting go of rules that are not important to your family. Just because a rule made sense when you came up with it, that doesn't mean it needs to stay written in stone forever.

If enforcing rules with a spouse seems too complicated, coparenting with a former spouse or significant other takes it to a whole new level. And that's before you even consider the fact that either you or they might be in a new relationship and there may be stepkids or half-siblings in the family too. Your relationship with the other parent probably ended because you two saw the world so differently, because of a deep hurt, or because you drifted apart and may not like each other very much at this point. But no matter the circumstances, the more you and the child's other parent can get on the same page with parenting, rules, and expectations, the better things will be *for your kids*. It takes a lot of extra work, and it will probably feel unfair at times. But remember, you're doing it for the kids!

Take the long view.

You might find yourself constantly wanting to give your kids anything they want. You might want to let them get away with things you know you probably shouldn't because it doesn't feel like that big of a deal. Or you may be tempted to try to remove every obstacle they face or to fix every pain point in their lives. But the truth is that overcoming obstacles and learning to be disciplined, even when they may not immediately see the reasoning behind it, is good for kids. In other words, it's important to reframe your perspective if you have some personal hangups about rules. If you think of them as "restrictions developed on a whim" by adults, then it's really important to retrain your own mind to understand that you're creating and enforcing rules because that's what's best for your kids.

That doesn't mean all the rules you design will be perfect. In fact, unintentionally doing things that harm our kids is a guaranteed part of being a parent. But if you get hung up on that, you will be paralyzed and unable to make any decisions or rules. When you realize you're putting rules in place because you're parenting with the long view, you'll be in a much better place.

If it makes you feel like "the bad guy" to create and enforce rules, then maybe thinking of things in a new way will help you.

If you don't enforce the rules, you're almost guaranteeing your kids will learn these important lessons from other people at some point in their lives—but at a far greater cost than if they learn them from you. If you choose to be a friend instead of a parent, you essentially set your kids up to learn things the hard way.

If you don't teach them to share, they'll probably learn that being selfish with their toys alienates them from the other kids at preschool. If you don't teach them to clean up after themselves, they'll probably learn that leaving messes behind alienates them from their roommates or spouse. If you don't teach them about discipline and hard work, they'll probably learn that it's hard for them to keep a job. Do you see what I'm getting at here? You might feel like you're doing the kind thing by not having or enforcing rules and teaching discipline, but you really aren't. This might strike you as harsh, but you're avoiding the responsibility of fully raising your kids. You're setting them up to learn some of these lessons from the people around them, who may or may not have their best interests at heart. If other kids don't want to be around your kids, they aren't likely to actually tell them why—and your kids won't even know that their bad attitude, selfishness, or impatience are why they can't make friends. Their bosses will probably be quicker to demote them or fire them than to start from scratch in teaching them the importance of being on time, treating customers right, and getting their work done.

The bottom line is that there are a lot of things your kids need to learn in order to function in the world, and it's your job to teach them. Obviously, no parent will do it perfectly, and every parent will have blind spots. But to fail to even try to teach those lessons in pursuit of being liked or thought of as "fun" is doing your kids a disservice. They may be happy in the meantime because they are allowed to play more video games than their friends or because they don't get in trouble for performing under their ability at school—but in the end, they will suffer.

When "Help" Isn't Helpful

It's important to understand that these challenges will show up in parenting in limitless ways. So many times, we work hard to do everything "right" and end up seeing that we accidentally had a negative impact on our kids. It's so easy to think *My parents did something wrong and it really impacted me, so I'm going to avoid doing that with my kids*. That's a completely normal and healthy thought, but it can result in the pendulum swinging too far to the other extreme. And going too far to the other extreme means the kids will run into *different* issues—not *fewer* issues.

Think about how this has played out in previous generations. Many parents of today's young adults were so-called "latch-key" kids. They came home from school to an empty house and were left in charge of themselves until a parent or guardian got home from work. Those kids grew up having to figure out how to solve their own problems. Many of them became adept at making dinner for themselves and maybe their siblings, too. They learned to do homework without a parent making sure they stayed on task.

To some, that lack of supervision might sound like a dream. But many of the kids who lived that experience, as they became parents themselves, swung pretty far to the other side of the pendulum. They became "helicopter" or "snowplow" parents. "Helicopter" parents are known for "hovering over" their kids and knowing all they can about everything in their lives. "Snowplow" parents are known for doing all they can to push any and all obstacles out of their kids' way.

These parents, often after having grown up fending for themselves, are bound and determined to be there for their kids. They show up to every sporting event, every school event, and every other extracurricular activity you can imagine. And that's great, but they also often heckle coaches and referees, blame teachers and school administrators, and blur the line between "helping" and "taking over" on science fair projects. Do you see how a desire to be an active and engaged parent can end up resulting in some missteps? If you parent like this and can't see it, the people around you sure can. This is what happens when the line between parent and friend gets blurred.

Work to find ways to be there for your kids without being so involved that you take away some of their agency. They still need opportunities to learn—sometimes even from their mistakes. Those lessons will be the most costly for them, but they also will be the most valuable!

Substance Use and Abuse

It can be hard to find the line between friend and parent when substance abuse is an issue. Substance use is increasingly common among young adults, and the legalization of marijuana in many states has added a layer of complexity for parents. Winning At Home is not an addictions-counseling center, so this section deals strictly with recreational use that may develop into dependency.

Dr. Peter Newhouse is the founder of our Winning At Home Family Wellness Center, and he has spent the past thirty years counseling individuals, couples, and families through a wide variety of challenges. He recently had some conversations about substance use with his adult children and wanted to share his experience:

> Parenting adult children is tough now that chemical use (whether alcohol or pot) is much more normal in their age group. For many young adults, it's normal, healthy, and even natural to use marijuana as a source of pleasure, or to relieve emotional or physical pain. It's no longer illegal, or inappropriate in their eyes, so they have no problems with it.
>
> I've talked with my adult children about what's right and what's wrong, why marijuana was illegal, why it's not now, and what the healthy, responsible, godly thing is for them to do. My wife, Shawn Maree, and I have been trying to walk that fine line of coming

alongside our kids to have real discussions, but being careful not to alienate them or push them away while we still communicate our concern about the long-term effects and damage we feel excessive use of pot or alcohol could do.

As you can guess, or as you may know from experience, that's a tough needle to thread! It's hard to talk about, and it's probably even harder to find middle ground when our perspectives are different. In addition to that, it's hard to stay on the same page as a couple while we discuss it with our kids.

We experienced this recently. My wife wanted to engage more with the kids than I did—she wanted to talk more, and she also wanted me to talk more. But I tend to talk less and listen more. I like to let the kids share their perspective. But Shawn Maree felt that I didn't engage enough and wasn't strong enough in sharing my concerns and thoughts. Because she did most of the talking, she felt like she was alone in the discussion. So this already-tough conversation ended up being rather divisive for us as a couple.

Tough conversations like this require lots and lots of listening and keeping an open heart and mind both with your kids and with your partner.

We wanted to include Peter and Shawn Maree's experience here because it's a perfect example of what it looks like to put these ideas into practice. Navigating substance use and abuse in today's world is tough; it would have been much easier for them to avoid the discussion and just let their kids do whatever seemed right to them without saying anything about it. It would have been more comfortable, and it would have helped them avoid some marital conflict. But instead, they chose to be parents first and friends second.

When your kids live under your roof, you have the option of making these rules and deciding what can or can't happen. When your kids are adults who no longer live with you, sharing your thoughts is still important, but the outcome is much different because you can't make rules anymore. You can still share your wisdom and life experience, though—and that leads us to our next point.

When You Don't Agree

When your kids are young, it almost feels weird to call conflict with them *disagreement*. Honestly, it's easy to fall into the reasoning of "because I'm the parent and I said so" when the kids are younger and push against the rules. But do your best to check yourself on that response. Because even though you have more information and more knowledge about reasoning and consequences than your young children do, they still have a perspective. That doesn't mean their feedback needs to hold as much weight as yours, but it does mean that you should remain open to hearing about things you may have missed. Kids will probably find inconsistencies in your rules, and they'll be happy to remind you of the times you have broken them yourself. In those moments, don't respond in anger, even though you might feel it; instead, let them know you hear them and you're thinking about what they said. Then share what you decide. It's okay to let your kids know you are the one who makes the final decision, but it's really helpful for them to know their thoughts are valuable to you.

If this is important when your kids are younger, it becomes exponentially more important as they get older. Teens are working through hormones and puberty while gaining freedom and responsibilities, and all those things combine to make them a whole lot more likely to resist rules and statements they don't agree with. They also are more likely to seemingly enjoy disagreements, and they will share their opinions with gusto. That's part of the process of growing up, so do your best to remember that you're the adult in the room.

One of my sons and I got into an argument when he was in his teen years. I don't remember who raised his voice first, but I do know that we were both yelling by the end of the conversation. Afterward, my wife said, "Wow, it was hard to tell who the adult was as I was watching you two." As much as it hurt to hear that, I knew she had a point. So I told her that the next time I was losing my cool, she should come over and tell me to go to my room.

Unfortunately, that happened. I was arguing with that same son a little while after that conversation when Jane stepped in and said, "Dan, you need to go to your room." I resisted and tried to justify that my behavior wasn't actually that bad. But she just repeated herself, and I knew she was right. As I started walking to the bedroom to take some time off to calm down, I saw the look of shock (and victory) on my son's face. That happened years ago, but I still remember it clearly!

I'm not necessarily suggesting that everybody use that approach, but I do think it's helpful to have a release valve in the heated moments. If you are married, you can ask your spouse to tap you on the shoulder or give some other kind of signal that tells you to calm down or back off. If you are a single parent, you're going to have to hold yourself accountable if you get too upset. But no matter what safeguard you put in place, it's important to find a way to press pause when things get too heated and you risk saying or doing something you will regret.

Closing Thoughts

Many people think being a parent first and a friend second means you need to always make firm and harsh decisions. That you need to be strong if you want to be respected. That was how my (Dan's) own dad behaved in my home as I was growing up, and it created an unpleasant environment. That doesn't mean you can't have rules or things you won't compromise on, but make sure to view your parent/child relationship in the same way as other relationships: there needs to be some give and take. Don't think that you're "losing" or "giving up too much" if you change a rule because you realize it isn't helpful or no longer makes sense. Instead, be open to feedback and change. That's not a weakness; that's what it looks like to be a good parent!

Don't see this in terms of black and white: you aren't either a parent or a friend to your kids. You are both. There will be times when you must make decisions and discipline them, and there will be times when your kids need you to give them a listening ear and a shoulder to cry on. There will be other times when your kids need you to be there for them in a playful and fun way.

To be honest, it's hard to know the right way to handle things sometimes. You may struggle to decide whether it's time to enforce a rule or to give a pass, or to hand out a light or harsh punishment. Making those types of decisions is much more an art than a science—and often there will be no such thing as a "right" or "wrong" decision. But it's important for you to stay aware of this tension between being a friend and being the responsible adult who has to make the hard choices—because you will have to make some tough, and unpopular, calls at many points along the way. In those moments, do your best not to be guilted or pressured into a decision. Instead, remember that you're going through a learning process yourself, and that will inevitably involve making mistakes and learning from them. That's okay. Stay encouraged, because being a parent is hard but important work!

CHAPTER 10

I LOVE YOU
NO MATTER WHAT

Dan Seaborn

The world is complicated, and well-intentioned people can completely disagree with one another. Obviously, as Christians, we believe there is such a thing as right and wrong. But if we're honest, we can tend to try to make a lot of things into black-and-white issues when they really aren't. On lots of issues, we can convince ourselves that "our side" has the moral high ground, but it's likely that people who think the exact opposite feel that way too.

Here are a few things people disagree about: politics, religion, gender and sexuality, race relations, COVID-19, abortion, capital punishment, gun control, and a *whole bunch* of other things. I'm sure we've all watched an argument devolve from being about the initial topic to being about the other person's intelligence, decency, or mistakes.

You or somebody you know has likely lost a relationship over disagreement about these things. However, the relationship probably was not actually severed by the disagreement itself, but by the way the disagreement was handled. I believe the people who often appear on TV or write articles that we read online are either on one of the extreme ends of the ideological spectrum—or are pretending to be so for ratings. When I talk to actual people, the lines are rarely as black-and-white as media would have you believe. The reality is that having conversations with actual people we know in real life will likely be *very* different from the conversations we hear on TV and online; typically, normal and reasonable people don't think or talk in terms of absolutes or "my side" vs. "your side."

If you watch your local news very long, you'd start to think it's dangerous to go outside, whether it's day or night. But when you actually live your life, you don't have the same experience of running into danger and scammers around every corner. It's important to identify the ways that media and conversations we have on social media don't reflect our real-life experiences. Because when we lose sight of that, we can have knee-jerk reactions (shaped by those experiences) to the things our kids are saying.

Unfortunately, the way we communicate has been seriously damaged over the past several years. Extreme voices have become more commonplace because it's far easier to get people to tune in to your TV station or website if you're consistently fanning the flames of anger, fear, or mistrust. And let's be honest, it's far easier to see this happening when the information is coming from people we disagree with. We clearly see that "their" mouthpieces are spreading fear or hatred or distortions, but we don't realize that basically *all* forms of media are doing this, because the incentives are out of whack: it's financially and influentially beneficial for people to amplify negative messages. While this chapter isn't about the current media and information ecosystem, that is an important backdrop for discussing disagreements with the people in our lives.

I believe most of these all-or-nothing perspectives on different topics only exist on the far extremes; if you have an open conversation with somebody you actually have some kind of a relationship with, you will find more common ground than you might expect. You likely have several people in your life who don't see the world the same way you do, and you each probably enter conversations with certain assumptions about each other. But if you put aside the assumptions and actually work on listening for the purpose of understanding what the other person is saying, it will make a big difference!

That doesn't mean you are likely to change each other's minds, but it does mean you can stop seeing your conversation partner as a bad person on the wrong end of the ideological spectrum and start seeing him as a well-intentioned person who sees the world differently than you do—or someone whose core values don't line up exactly with yours. The bottom line is that lots of people are just wired differently than you are. Have you ever looked at your kids and wondered how it's possible that they have any genetic material in common with each other? Or with you? When they're our kids, our knee-jerk reaction isn't to write them off (like it might be with *that* neighbor or coworker), but to teach them to see things more like we do. There are times when that is helpful and appropriate, and times when it is not. Think of how many parents have tried to live vicariously through their kids and have steered them toward their own passions and interests rather than letting their kids guide that process by expressing theirs. A lot of kids are playing a sport because their parent never got to, or at least didn't achieve what they wanted to in it.

Because if your first thought when you hear your kids express an opposing viewpoint to yours is to think that nobody with that viewpoint is a decent human being, you may be heading down the road to a conversation that will do some damage to your relationship. That's not to say you have to sit passively and not share your perspective. But it's important that you remember that the relationship is the top priority—not complete agreement.

If you feel yourself getting triggered or defensive in a conversation with your kids (or anyone else), it's okay to say you'd like to change the topic because you don't have the mental or emotional energy for that one. If you try to push through and emotion takes over the conversation, the chance of somebody saying something they regret increases significantly because these are emotionally charged topics. The way the topics are discussed on a regular basis can either add or subtract fuel from the fire.

The Solution

The rest of the chapter will contain bullet points of some simple and practical tips on the topic of disagreement, discord, and conflict. But the fact that the tips themselves are simple doesn't mean they will be easy to implement! It takes work to put them into practice, but the effort will be worth it for your relationships.

I want to start this list with a reminder of what the Apostle Paul wrote about love in 1 Corinthians 13:4–8:

> Love is patient, love is kind. It does not envy, it does not boast, it is not proud. It does not dishonor others, it is not self-seeking, it is not easily angered, it keeps no record of wrongs. Love does not delight in evil but rejoices with the truth. It always protects, always trusts, always hopes, always perseveres. Love never fails.

If we keep this description of love as our goal in our tough conversations, we'll see a whole different outcome!

Seek unity, not complete agreement.

If we're aiming for complete agreement, we're going to be disappointed time and again. Using that as the bar for success will mean we're almost guaranteed to fall short.

It's a given that you and your family won't always see things in the same way. Of course, you will probably agree about most things, but there will definitely be differences. Some of them will be minor, while some will be more significant. But it's important that we all try to respect each other along the way and remember that we're aiming for unity. That means even when we don't see eye-to-eye, we work to avoid outbursts and big arguments about the best approach to the situation. No family will do this perfectly, but don't get discouraged. Keep working at it!

Let your kids know you really love them— no matter what!

This will be greatly beneficial—especially when you completely disagree on important things and perhaps even end up parting ways for a while. In Romans 8:38–39, Paul writes this about God's love for us:

> For I am convinced that neither death nor life, neither angels nor demons, neither the present nor the future, nor any powers, neither height nor depth, nor anything else in all creation, will be able to separate us from the love of God that is in Christ Jesus our Lord.

As parents, we'll fall short of responding perfectly every time, but we can commit to the principle here that *nothing* can stop us from loving our kids. We can reflect God in that way as we love our kids *no matter what.*

Don't feed into drama; neutralize it!

Our society loves drama. We seem to be hardwired to find people who think like we do and to oppose people who don't.

If we're not careful, this societal trend of escalating disagreements and conflicts can become a habit in our daily lives. Escalating only makes things worse, but it's easy to do when emotions are involved, or when we misunderstand somebody and make assumptions about their motives.

Oddly enough, this is especially hard to do in conversations with our loved ones. Because we have much more of a history with them and know their weak points as well as they know ours, difficult conversations with our families are more likely to escalate than our conversations with coworkers or neighbors. In addition, we also feel like we have "permission" to lose our temper with our families because we know they love us and are likely to forgive us. Instead of treating the people who love us most more poorly than we treat other people, let's make sure to practice de-escalation in our intimate relationships first!

Move on instead of holding on.

One of the things my wife is especially good at is moving on. I probably notice that because I'm not nearly as good at it. I tend to hang on to stuff like slights, frustrations, annoyances, or disagreements. I want to talk about things I should just let go because I want to hash them out. That's my nature. When something goes wrong or is frustrating or difficult, I hang on to it and wind up having multiple conversations to try to process what happened, what could have been different, and why it was so hard for me.

Tenacity is also one of my strengths, and it serves me well in lots of situations. I can push through when others would give in. But it definitely has some downsides, and this tendency is one of them. If you resonate with this, I hope to help you see you may be ruminating on things that aren't worth spending much time thinking about.

This is still pretty new for me. But lately, I've been making a concerted effort to let things go more often—and I've found more peace and contentment as I stop replaying things in my head and work to move past them.

Remember that our tendency to create "teams" is natural.

We clearly live in a world that loves to create divisions and make it known who's in and who's out. The way our brains work lends itself to this. It's kind of a shortcut so that we don't have to think deeply about every single situation that arises. And for the most part, it's actually helpful. When we were young, we could put our parents or siblings into the category of "trusted" people, which dramatically simplified life, because if Mom or Dad said something, we knew we could trust that information and act on it. Over time, we learned that life isn't actually that simple, and we all felt the disappointment of realizing that somebody we trusted had given us some wrong information. Or worse, maybe they manipulated or took advantage of us.

We live in a world where every topic is now hotly debated because we've lost trust in lots of people and sources of information. That has made it much more natural for each of us to dig in deep on the things that are important to us. Some of those things are genuinely important, but we've all probably found ourselves getting far too riled up about something that, in a moment when cooler heads prevailed, we would admit we didn't actually care about *that* much. Another way this shows up is when people fall short, we view negative consequences they might face as them "getting what they deserve." In her book *Bittersweet*, Shauna Niequist writes honestly about how she responded to a friend who had hurt her:

> [S]he asked for my advice, many years ago, and went against it. This situation wouldn't exist had she taken my advice. So now my small, ugly self doesn't want to pray for her.[1]

That hits a little too close to home, doesn't it? It's natural to be way too quick to put somebody on the opposite team and to push them further away when we've decided they aren't "with" us. Don't allow yourself to do this with your kids, no matter what. Instead, keep fighting to love them!

---

[1] Shauna Niequist, *Bittersweet* (Grand Rapids, MI: Zondervan, 2010), 82.

Don't make certain questions or topics off-limits.

The internet connects people in ways that are both amazing and scary. Because there are so many different options, and we can connect with anyone, it has become much more normal for us to leave a conversation, stop visiting a website, or mute or unfollow somebody's feed if they say something we strongly disagree with.

I'm not interested in trying to convince you to spend huge amounts of your time interacting online with people you deeply disagree with. But I point this out because I think it's having a secondary effect on many of our personal relationships. You can only practice "tuning out" of a conversation you disagree with for so long before it becomes second nature.

Our interactions with loved ones should be as far from the "online comment section" experience as possible! But I fear many of us aren't as intentional as we need to be about allowing our spouse and kids to freely express their thoughts and ideas. I'll warn you up front: Your teen might share something, and your immediate reaction will be, "That's wrong!" You'll be tempted to shut the conversation down, but do your best to resist that impulse.

It's important to give your children the freedom to express their thoughts, frustrations, and confusions about life because that will help them realize, "Wow! My home is a safe place to let all of me out." A huge bonus is that you will be able to share your perspective so that your kids aren't getting most of their information about how life works from their classmates or their favorite YouTuber. When you're willing to hear their thoughts, even when you don't agree, they can grow and learn from you.

Sarah Ingram, a counselor who used to work with us at Winning At Home, told me about a few key (and difficult!) steps to create an environment in which your child knows he can talk with you about anything. She said that no matter what he's saying, do your best to keep your facial expressions and mannerisms from changing. That means your arms don't cross and you don't make your "exasperated face." Instead, she told me to work hard to respond with, "Thanks for telling me that" even when you're screaming internally. Obviously, this is really hard! But it opens the door for our kids to know they can come to us with anything. Even though we won't necessarily agree, they won't feel judged or shunned for bringing something up to you.

Speak kindly.

For the most part, people do a good job of regulating themselves in a professional or public setting. Some do it better than others, but for the most part, it's fairly uncommon to see an adult lose their temper in most public places. We know we have to be "on" in those settings.

Unfortunately, when we're at home, we know we can relax and just be ourselves, which is a good thing overall. But sometimes we "relax" in areas where we shouldn't. We may stop speaking kindly and responding gently because we're sick of doing all that work. Lots of people justify this in strange ways. You may have heard somebody say, "They already know I love them" as an excuse to speak sharply to their spouse and family. You may have seen people who are friendly and full of smiles when they're in public but who do a whole lot of yelling and demeaning behind closed doors.

In light of the differences we sometimes see between people's public and private lives, I'd like to challenge you to work on your own "behind closed doors" moments. Can you relate to being kinder and gentler with your neighbors or coworkers than with your spouse and kids? If so, commit to making a change. I know the relationships aren't the same. But I also know that it's not fair for everybody except for your family to get to interact with the best version of you.

Watch your tone.

When we're tired, annoyed, or stressed, it's easy to let exasperation and frustration creep into our tone. It might not change the volume of our words, but it definitely changes the way they feel to the person you're talking with. Start there. Pay attention to *how* you're saying what you're saying. Remember that the exact same words can convey completely different meanings depending on your tone—they could come across as sincere, neutral, sarcastic, or defensive. That's why speaking gently and sincerely has such a positive impact on relationships.

Also, when hard or negative emotions are involved, try to speak at half the volume you would naturally use. Volume communicates more than we realize sometimes, and reining this in can be really helpful. If you need to work on these things, don't beat yourself up if you mess up. You're doing something new, and that always takes time and practice!

Watching my tone and working to speak kindly and gently has made a huge difference in my life! When I don't do it, misunderstandings and hurt feelings abound. When I do it, I see my relationships flourish. I trust you'll have a similar experience.

Be a peacemaker.

Most of us know there are a significant number of topics that are off-limits if our goal is to have a pleasant conversation. Lately, I've been thinking a lot about whether I am a "peacemaker" or "peace-taker." One of the ways to determine this is to ask yourself, "Do people get excited when they see me coming their way?" If you're a "peace-taker," the answer is often "no." Work to be a peacemaker in your family.

A Place of Peace?

Your home should not be a battle zone. Somebody reading this might be thinking, "Well, mine is!" And I get that. There are times where there will be conflict in our homes—that's just life. But you don't want it to be that way all the time. As a parent, you must do everything you can to make sure your home doesn't become a battle zone.

I fully understand that's easier said than done. My wife and I struggled to figure out how to do this, especially when our kids were in their teens. When kids want independence and identity outside of the family, it really feels like there could be a battle every time they walk through the door. But you have to decide you're not going to let it come to that.

One way to do that is by working to avoid having the same argument over and over, especially when both sides know that changing anybody's opinion is extremely unlikely. Another way is to do your best to squash bickering and teasing when it starts rather than allowing it to continue until it devolves into a big blowup.

We didn't do this perfectly! We had ongoing arguments as well as pestering and bickering that turned into bigger issues. But we worked hard to make sure that these types of interactions didn't become the norm in our home—and when we ran into those issues, we made it clear that the goal was to work toward peace and kindness.

That obviously doesn't mean you won't have conflict and disagreements. Those things are bound to happen in any deep relationship. You'll have some tough discussions, and you'll have to figure out how to grow through them. But it's important that those conversations are not the normal way you communicate in your home. Instead, come up with ways to make sure the typical tone used is positive, encouraging, and uplifting.

Assume the best.

In general, people don't set out to be mean or wicked. They don't plot the best way to ruin somebody's day when they wake up in the morning. Of course, there are exceptions, but those are few and far between. Most people are just looking to get by, and when they do things that hurt other people, it's generally out of inattention rather than malice. And that's especially important to remember when it comes to the people in your family.

When there is conflict or frustration, it's easy to start thinking the other person is out to get you. That they're doing something on purpose in order to hurt you. Let's stop and think about that for a moment. When was the last time you assumed malicious intent rather than inattention? Typically, we go into that mode when somebody in our family misses something that is completely obvious to us. And because we care so much about the look of the car, lawn, bathroom, or kitchen, our family's lack of follow-through jumps out at you the second you see it.

Let's work on giving our kids the benefit of the doubt when something isn't done according to our plan or preference. Let's assume they have a different perspective than we do or a blind spot when it comes to a certain task or chore. If you can take the time to go through this thought process before you respond or react, I truly believe it will have a positive impact on the way you view your family.

Respond in love.

A loving response will always win. I'm not saying that responding in love will always feel good, but it will always be better for the relationship. It won't always be easy, and it will require sacrifice and surrender from us because there will always be the temptation to make our point or put somebody in their place and say, "I told you so!"

When you have an opportunity to throw out some fiery language or say something you know will be cutting and hurtful, love will win. I'll be the first to admit that an angry, sarcastic, or cutting response can feel good. But it will only feel good for a short time. Harsh words have negative consequences—we all know that. The problem is that when our emotions are heightened, it's difficult to think clearly. When we're angry, ashamed, or hurt, a harsh response feels appropriate. But love, kindness, and caring will be the things that strengthen a relationship. Harsh responses tear it down.

Remember that words can hurt.

You've probably heard people talk about the idea of words being "heavy" or "carrying weight." Part of the reason these images carry so much meaning is because we've all had the experience of feeling crushed by someone's words. As we get older, we realize that the playground phrase, "Sticks and stones may break my bones, but words will never hurt me" is well-meaning but incorrect. It's good because it helps kids learn to let some things roll off their backs. But it's not accurate because we all know that words can definitely hurt us.

Like anybody else, I've heard hurtful things in close relationships. When that happened, I did my best to look like they hadn't wounded me. But on the inside, I felt crushed. That's a feeling I'm sure we all know too well—because words have a surprising way of cutting through our defenses and causing pain, whether they're describing something true about us or not.

I grew up watching my mom get crushed by words quite often, and she didn't say anything about it, and I saw how it changed her. After years of bearing the brunt of my dad's negative and hurtful words, I saw her slowly switch roles with him. As he aged, he became quieter and gentler, which was the role that my mom had been in for years. But as she aged, she became more impatient and frustrated, which was the role that my dad had played.

Watching that play out in my parents' relationship really helped me understand the importance of speaking up when I'm on the receiving end of hurtful words. I watched the transformation that can happen if you don't say anything and just try to ignore the hurt or push it down and keep going. Instead of doing that, I want to encourage all of us to stop pretending that "words will never hurt" us. Because they can. And they do.

So let's commit to speaking up and working to strengthen our relationships. When we let people know how their words are impacting us, we create an opportunity for the relationship to grow.

CHAPTER 11

PARENTING ADULT CHILDREN

Dan Seaborn and Dr. Peter Newhouse

N avigating the changes in a relationship during your child's transition from teenager into adulthood is neither simple nor straightforward; in fact, it's surprisingly hard. After all the hands-on, all-in work parenting requires through the first sixteen to twenty years of a child's life, suddenly letting them go produces some whiplash. If you're having a hard time walking that fine line, know you're not alone.

Before we dive into that discussion, allow me to say that if you're married and you and your spouse are in the process of becoming empty-nesters, you have the additional challenge of working through how that will impact your marriage. Many couples find that their kids have been their main focus and they have drifted apart from one another. Others find that they no longer have many personal hobbies or interests for the same reason. Some marriages end after the kids leave home because the "buffer" between the spouses disappears. That won't be the focus of this chapter, but it's an important aspect that catches many parents off guard.

Just as when they were growing up, I've found that each of my four adult kids are wired differently and need different things from me. Alan has always been more independent and prefers his own space. Josh has always been relational and interested in diving deep into the things he cares about. Crissy has always been energetic and ready to get involved in whatever is happening around her. Anna has always been thoughtful and deeply committed to what is important to her.

Obviously, these distinctions aren't meant to fully describe or define my kids; I'm just trying to help you get a sense of how those four approaches to life differ, and how they can result in family conflict. That hasn't changed over the years. What has changed significantly is how I handle my involvement in these moments. When the kids were growing up, I would take a much more active role in helping each of them navigate their relationships with each other. These days, I'm still involved in that, but I do a lot less mediation than I once did because they're all adults and they can figure it out.

My oldest son Alan contributed to the chapter "Handling Technology Well." I asked him to share a brief story here to describe one particular moment from his perspective:

> I bought my first home when I was single and had recently moved back to the area where I grew up. The house needed several repairs, and I was having to pick and choose which projects to prioritize with my limited budget. My dad helped me paint the walls and finish the floors, so he definitely did a lot of good along the way. But the main thing I remember about his involvement was when he took matters into his own hands. He decided that the next thing I should spend my limited funds on was the garage door opener. There was a unit installed, but it didn't work. And nobody in my family is mechanically inclined, so this was a repair that definitely needed to be hired out. That was probably fix number ten or fifteen on my priority list at the time. I had been parking my car outside for years at that point, so the idea of a garage was nice, but not pressing.
>
> Dad knew a guy who worked on garage doors, so he called him to come fix it without telling me. The way I see it, my dad spent $500 of *my money* on something that wasn't a priority for me, and I let him know that. I didn't know how fully my point had hit home

until I called him a couple weeks later looking for help. I was having a hard time getting my lawnmower to start. When I finished describing the issue I was having, he said, "Well, what are you calling *me* for?" When we hung up, we were both mad.

Walking that fine line can be really hard, can't it? Probably nearly every parent of an adult child can relate. We want to help, and we want to be involved. Just like we've done their whole lives, we want to prevent our kids from learning lessons the hard way, so we're constantly tempted to jump in and take over! From Alan's description of what happened, you may feel it's unfair that his main memory of that time was the moment when I overstepped rather than the hours I spent on the painting and flooring. And you're right. He and I both agree it's not fair to minimize all that work to focus on that one situation—but that's the tricky nature of memory, and it shows how powerful negative experiences can be.

This story fits well in this chapter because every family will have experiences like this. That's just part of life. But the goal of parenting is to figure out how to navigate this complexity well and to learn to bless and encourage our kids as they move into adulthood. We want to help them learn to grow and mature in ways that are not only biblical, but also functional and that contribute to maturity in all areas of life.

As you can already see, launching kids well requires a lot of emotional work from the parents because you're learning new skills at this stage. Just as you had to learn how to change diapers and soothe crying babies and navigate teenage challenges and mood swings, now you have to learn how to let go and release them—and part of that is learning not to take the loss and change personally. Our ultimate job is to help our kids make great choices and be independent. In other words, we're working ourselves out of the job we've had for decades. The ultimate goal of parenting is to make sure they are not dependent on us, they don't need us to step in to fix things, and they're able to live without us.

Of course, there will be a major learning curve on both sides of the relationship, and there are bound to be hurt feelings and misunderstandings along the way. Try to remember that your kids are new at this, too! After many awkward (and maybe painful) moments, you'll start to get a better feel for the new dynamic of your relationship, and you'll see opportunities to speak into their lives and help them as adults in a more hands-off way. It's definitely not a simple process; it's actually very challenging and complex. But it's important, and it's worth it!

In this section, Dr. Peter Newhouse will share directly from a clinical perspective.

> I think kids often feel a lot of pressure to take care of their parents and to meet their emotional needs. That can be a lot of pressure, depending on the child and his personality. A lot of times those adult children feel like they can't individuate. They feel like if they truly

branch out and become their own person, it will hurt or devastate their parents.

So really learning to let go is not only for your own mental and emotional health as a parent, but also for that adult child who is trying to figure out his own world, his own life, and his own needs. It's important at this stage to work to make it clear that different is not bad. Make it clear that you expect your child to have different thoughts, feelings, and values than you do—just as we have from our parents. Allow the kids to figure that out and feel safe to pursue their own values, thoughts, and feelings, and to be who God has called them to be.

Winning At Home is based in a small, tight-knit community in West Michigan. People sometimes refer to Hope College, our local school, as "13th Grade" because so many people strongly expect to stay in the area and do all they can to live near their parents. There's absolutely nothing wrong with adults growing up and living in or near their hometown—as long as they're doing it because that's what they want and they feel that's where God is leading them. But if they're doing it because of pressure or expectations from their parents, that's a whole different conversation. Please be vigilant for signs of this showing up in your own parenting and work to correct that.

I (Dan) have some experience with this myself. Today, all four of my adult children live in West Michigan within a twenty- to twenty-five-minute drive from the home where Jane and I live. But it hasn't always been like that. Josh, our second-born, lived states away with his family for many years, but recently moved back to our area. Having that distance between us was a letting-go process all its own, and I'm sure many people reading this can relate. It was hard for Jane and me to live so far away from the grandkids that we would have loved to see much more often than we did over those years! But it reminds us of our own journey with our parents when we first were married.

I grew up in South Carolina and Jane grew up in North Carolina. Early in our marriage, we moved to Michigan and have now lived here for over thirty years. That meant our kids didn't get to know their grandparents the same way that Jane and I had known ours, but it was part of our journey as we sought to be faithful to God's leading and calling on our lives.

No matter how close or how far you are from family, some things will be key for every relationship. Here are three ways that Peter suggests we can effectively release our adult children and walk that fine line of staying involved without being overinvolved:

Be available, but give space.

This is hard. As we mentioned before, some of the skills you need for parenting adult children are almost the *opposite* of what you needed as they were growing up! You're used to doing things on your terms as a parent, but as they grow up and become adults, you must increasingly shift to their terms. Parents are used to being in control and dictating the rules, boundaries, and expectations. It's key that we allow that balance to shift and give space to let our adult children control their own lives. This is especially hard when they do something we disagree with, or that we don't think they've fully thought through.

Be flexible with everything.

The adults you raised now have their own lives and their own responsibilities. Here's a brief snapshot of what they're responsible for now: How they raise their kids, how they pay their bills, what they eat, how they view the world—in other words, pretty much everything. Be flexible with how they want to do the big things and the little things, even their faith journey. I know it's anxiety-inducing and maybe even painful to watch them live out their faith differently than you think they should, but give them space to do things their way—just as you wanted your parents to do for you.

Be patient.

It's easy to jump to conclusions or assume the worst, especially in areas where you disagree with your kids. Instead of being reactive or frustrated, extend a lot of grace and patience. Patience isn't natural for any of us, but that's especially true when it comes to our relationship with our kids. This is even more of a challenge if our young adult children are going in an unhealthy direction. However, the truth of the matter is that you can't force them to change or make different decisions, and trying to do so will just result in conflict and anger.

These three points are all geared toward one thing: maintaining the relationship no matter what. In the next section, we'll talk about broken relationships.

Toxicity, a New Way of Thinking

You've probably at least heard about a parent who has had the heartbreaking experience of a child cutting them out of their lives. The trend of people cutting "toxic" people out of their lives is growing. From my parents' generation to my kids', the standard for what is considered "toxic" has changed immensely, and it's made parenting a lot more complicated. You probably think of a "toxic" person as somebody who has been sexually or physically abusive, but for many younger people, that definition falls short of what they're thinking. This also applies to the way they define "trauma."

Unfortunately, the American ideal of "individualism" has some poisonous side effects. "If *I* am the main focus and point of life, then whatever causes me pain or discomfort is something I should reevaluate in terms of net gain and loss." This is what a lot of young people today are being encouraged to do. But the problem is that all close relationships involve moments of pain and disagreement—in fact, those things are necessary for increased depth.

Prioritizing the Relationship

The goal is to keep the relationship alive—no matter what. One of the ways to strain a relationship, or even push it to the breaking point, is to insist on having things your way. Or to insist that everybody share your thoughts, opinions, and values. Again, this is strange because up to now, you've been the one to set the rules in your relationship with your kids. But now it's time to value the relationship over rules.

As I've mentioned previously, I (Dan) grew up in a home with very strict rules. My mom wasn't allowed to wear pants, use makeup, or cut her hair. I wasn't allowed to play organized sports or attend games. We couldn't have a TV or go to the movies. Even after I had moved out and had my own family, whenever I would go back to visit my parents, I would stop the car about a mile from their house, change out of my shorts and put on pants, because my dad didn't think adults should wear shorts—even in South Carolina in the spring. Coming from Michigan, it usually felt like a mid-summer day! Think about that for a moment: I was a thirty-year-old adult changing the clothes I would normally wear because I knew how to do the song and dance my dad would require of me. Today's kids are less likely to submit to unreasonable requests like this, which is actually a good thing! (Of course, that can go too far, and they can ignore things that actually are important.)

When you're tempted to jump in and impose your standards on your kids, try to remember your own journey into adulthood and independence. What was your perspective on being parented when you were twenty, twenty-five, and thirty? When you try to see things from their point of view and make the effort to remember what this transition was like for you, it will help you to be sensitive to where they are in life.

Parenting young adults will be unpredictable. As we mentioned earlier, every one of your kids is different and will have different needs and desires in terms of involvement from their parents as they move out of the house and establish their independence. Add to that the fact that geographic distance, different views, and the people they date and marry will further add to the complexity. Despite all the surprises and unpredictability, some things are universal:

- We all want to be loved and accepted.
- We all want to be affirmed.
- We all want to be spoken to kindly.
- We all want our parents to be proud of us. In other words, parents' voices will continue to matter.

Knowing that these are the basics of any relationship reminds us that even as lots of the details of the relationship are changing, the core components are still the same. One way to navigate those changes is to develop a strategy for parenting young adults. It will help to come up with a plan for when and where to intervene (and when not to) ahead of time rather than trying to make those decisions in the heat of the moment. This also helps define the key principles that really matter and where you need to take a strong stance.

Whether you're at this stage and your kids are already adults, or if you're working to prepare yourself and your expectations ahead of time, it's important to understand that this is a new phase of parenting. Just as there's an adjustment period when young kids start walking or start school, there's an adjustment period when your adult children leave the home and start building a life centered around new friends, significant others, jobs, and priorities. That might sound threatening or negative to you, but it's important to remember that *this is the whole goal of parenting!* You invested in your kids for decades and taught them about responsibility and morality to prepare them for independence and the freedom to make their own decisions.

Hopefully, you had some strategies for staying connected as your kids were growing up. Maybe you had a weekly family game or movie night or a monthly night out as a family. You had strategies for other seasons of your kids' lives, and now your strategies must evolve to meet the needs of the current moment. Here are a few ways these strategies can change with your kids' ages and needs:

- When your kids were young, maybe you read or prayed with them at mealtime or bedtime. For your adult kids, maybe you regularly send them a "Verse of the Week" or a note of encouragement.
- When your kids were young, you had ultimate control over how you celebrated holidays or family

time. For your adult kids, you need to be much more flexible and give them freedom to decide how they want to celebrate. This becomes even more important when they have a significant other or a spouse and are splitting their time between two families of origin.

• When your kids were young, you found ways to engage in their interests with them. You probably watched one movie or show over and over, or played with blocks or dolls when you actually were not interested at all. For some strange reason, it's easy to stop actively engaging with your kids' interests as they get older. But try to find a way to connect—even if you feel silly or think you'd just be holding them back if you asked to tag along.

I (Peter) get calls from parents almost weekly to talk about their concerns and fears. I just got off a call with a parent of an adult child who was going through a situation that left the parent feeling out of control and scared. I regularly hear some version of the following phrases: "My child is going wayward," "I am really sad about the lifestyle choices he is making," "I need help," "What do I do?" "How do I/we intervene?" "Do we do an intervention with all his siblings, or do my husband and I just meet with you to talk?" These questions, and many more, are common among parents of adult children who feel at a loss and don't know how to respond to a situation they're facing. They're not sure how to engage or how to help. Parents regularly tell me they just want to share all their concerns; they don't think their child has any idea what is going on with them and how hurt, sad, and worried they are about their life and choices.

Here are some of the words people use to describe what it feels like to parent adult children: "difficult," "painful," "complicated," "messy," "ugly," and "scary."

The stakes get higher as children get older. The consequences of choices and actions are far greater and more permanent—including pregnancy, dating or marrying somebody that the family doesn't like, or having a criminal record.

Launching Adult Kids as a Single Parent

As hard as this change is to navigate for two-parent families, it's often even more challenging for single-parent families. You're dealing with things that those of us who are in two-parent families don't even understand. You've probably developed a uniquely close relationship with your kids, and letting them go is especially painful. As you go through this phase, make sure to connect with other parents who are going or have been through it as well. It's very helpful to have other people to bounce ideas off, as well as to share in your victories and defeats along the way. No matter how many challenges you've successfully navigated on your own, it will be particularly beneficial for you to have a support system around you for this one.

Staying United as a Couple

As we (Dan and Peter) talk with couples about launching their kids into adulthood, we think it's absolutely vital that they pray together and stay united. And by "united," we don't mean that they think and feel exactly the same. We all know from personal experience that we won't always respond the same way as our spouse. Instead, we encourage parents to communicate with each other in addition to spending time in prayer. These are two key pieces as you work to stay on the same page about how to deal with and manage this young adults' behaviors, attitudes, and choices.

It's easy to talk about being united in a marriage, but really *being* united and talking through difficult things as a couple, especially divisive, painful things, is hard. Usually one of the parents (often the mom) really wants to intervene and deal with the child's behavior. They want to pull that child aside, sit them down, and talk it through. The other parent (often the dad) wants to be more passive—to take a more hands-off approach and let the kid figure it out. Having such different philosophies about how to approach a situation complicates things right out of the gate. And to make things even more complex, there's usually not a right or wrong answer—it's more of the parents landing on a point where they can be united and agree upon an approach in general. Both are worried about the child's well-being and long-term health. Often, they're both worried, in different ways, about driving a wedge between that child and themselves, or pushing them away from themselves or God. These are tough issues, and it's hard to know how to intervene or how the intervention will affect that adult child.

Staying United When Blended

Whether you're married, single, or remarried, having two healthy parents involved in raising kids is absolutely the preferred situation—even when that means your kids are learning to live between two households and adjusting to new stepparents and stepsiblings. Obviously, these situations are very challenging for most people, because you often have emotional responses surrounding your child's other parent—and after breakups or divorces, former spouses or partners usually know how to push each other's buttons!

So what does it look like to "stay united" in a situation like that? The three rules Peter mentioned earlier in this chapter will continue to be a great guide: (1) be available, but give space, (2) be flexible with everything, and (3) be patient. I understand it will be very challenging at times not to get angry or defensive, but if you can remember that both you and your kids' other parent want what's best for them and to set them up for success, it'll go a long way toward staying united. It's hard to give the benefit of the doubt and to believe the best about somebody when we're frustrated with them, but do all you can to approach your interactions with that understanding.

Praying Parents

We'll close this chapter by looking at a few of the reasons praying for your kids is so important. Prayer isn't last because it's an afterthought, but because we want it to be the takeaway and application as we finish this difficult topic. After reading through this list of just a few of the benefits of prayer, we hope you'll take some time to apply these truths and pray for your kids, no matter what stage of life they're in!

Prayer helps me realize I might be wrong, and that's okay.

This one is first on the list for a reason. It's easy to think of ourselves as experienced and wise, which would make our opinions and perspectives the *right* ones. But when we take the time to put ourselves in the appropriate position of asking God for His wisdom and leading, we're reminded that we're not as wise and all-knowing as we may sometimes like to think we are.

It gives a bigger perspective and gets me out of my immediate focus.

Similarly, when we cast our cares on God, we are often reminded of the fact that His work and His Kingdom are so much bigger than we're remembering in a moment when we're weighed down by some of the heavy things going on in our lives and in our family.

It helps me let go of (or at least loosen up on) my agenda.

We can't continue to pray like Jesus taught—"Your Kingdom come, Your will be done on Earth as it is in Heaven"—if we are actually laser-focused on our will being done! Hopefully, our desires in these moments are for our kids to make choices that honor God rather than to follow our traditions. Spending time in honest prayer will help us see those differences.

It reminds me that my child is not mine, but God's.

When we spend time in prayer, we're reminded that God loves our child more than we do. That's hard to wrap our minds around (it almost seems offensive, doesn't it?), but it's true. God's love for our kids is above and beyond even our capacity.

It gives me patience and calmness, because it reminds me it doesn't all rest on my shoulders.

As 1 Peter 5:7 tells us, we can cast all our cares on Him because He cares for us. This doesn't mean we will immediately stop feeling anxious or having a preference about any given situation, but that anxiety can remind us to stop and hand things back over to God.

It helps remind me that my spouse or my child is pretty great overall.

One of the most surprising aspects of prayer is that it's hard to stay mad at somebody while you're praying for them, because prayer is intentionally inviting God into the moment and asking for His peace and strength. When we do that, it's nearly impossible to stay mad at the person we're praying for, even if we continue to be hurt or disappointed.

It helps me remember that the situation is only temporary.

Calling on our eternal God puts the timeframe in perspective as well. As God reminded Job, we weren't there at the point of creation, and He's the one who knows the depths of the sea or the heights of the mountains. God always sees a bigger picture than we do.

It helps me see that I did my best as a parent, and so did my spouse.

Calling on God and asking for His help and grace also naturally allows us to be more gracious with ourselves and with the people we care deeply about. This time will help us to forgive ourselves and our spouse for the moments when we didn't handle things well. Likely, no specific situation in our parenting past did as much damage to our child as we may have thought.

It helps me remember my child is an adult who is responsible for his choices.

In a similar vein, prayer reminds us that much of the responsibility we've been taking is actually not ours to bear. As kids age, we stop being able to force them to do certain things, and they get to make their own choices. This is a painful process, but part of their freedom involves dealing with the outcomes of those choices, whether negative or positive.

Take some time to pray for each of your kids (and their families, if applicable). Ask God to help you know where to step in and where to step back. Ask Him to help you be gracious and loving, even when there is tension and conflict. Ask Him to work in each of your kids' lives as they go their own way and make their own choices.

CONCLUSION

We hope that every chapter in this book has provided you with simple, practical, and helpful insights. There are already many books about each of the topics we covered—so if any of these chapters piqued your interest, they can serve as a launch pad for you to dig deeper.

As you work to apply the things you've read, you'll notice the areas where you need more input or strategy. When you reach that point, please take the time to look into some of the other great resources tackling these topics from a biblical perspective. Whether you're looking for more insight on healthy communication, navigating mental health concerns, or addressing sexuality- or gender-related questions, there are resources available. Please don't feel like you're alone as you navigate some of these exceptionally challenging aspects of parenting. Many other parents are struggling to figure out the best way forward right along with you.

You can learn many things about your specific situation through books or websites, listening to sermons or podcasts, or talking with other parents. But please don't forget one of the most important sources of information about your children—talking with *them* about what they're going through! You know your own kids better than any third party will, so you're in a great position to know how to best come alongside them as they struggle and grow.

Sometime when you're genuinely open to feedback, ask them if they know what they need from you, what they want to get out of life, or where there's a disconnection between what they're thinking and what you're thinking. That type of openness can help deepen your relationship with them as well as your mutual trust. As with all relationships, you will need to continually put time, effort, and energy into developing your relationship with each of your kids—but as you continue to invest in them and follow God's leading as a family, I believe you'll be Winning at Home!

ABOUT THE CONTRIBUTORS

Dan Seaborn is the founder of Winning At Home and an engaging and powerful speaker. He has a comfortable, humorous communication style that allows him to connect easily with audiences of all ages. Dan talks openly about family life, often through revealing his own struggles or failures. As the featured speaker at various large-scale events all over the country, Dan has earned recognition as an influential and passionate communicator who uses practical illustrations and real-life examples to teach others how to win at home.

Dr. Emilie DeYoung has a doctorate in psychology with an emphasis on child and adolescent counseling, and a master's degree in social work. She has been working with children and families since 1996. Specific areas of expertise include childhood anxiety disorders, obsessive-compulsive disorder, depression, attention deficit hyperactivity disorder, childhood temperament, and trauma recovery. In a casual and relational style, Emilie strives to help kids and teens understand their value. With contemporary interventions, she helps families remove the barriers that prevent them from reaching their full potential.

Alan Seaborn is a pastor and author. He is committed to helping bring harmony to parent-child relationships. Through stories from Scripture and the world around him, he shares about the things that are close to God's heart—our attitudes and the decisions we make—all viewed through the lens of a family relationship.

Brad Klaver is the coaching director for Winning At Home. With nearly fifteen years of pastoral care and coaching experience, he is a highly relational, outside-the-box thinker. Brad holds certifications in leadership coaching and mental health coaching. He loves to provide pastoral care for individuals, married couples, parents, and teams from a Spirit-led, biblically rooted foundation. Additionally, he works with individuals and families who are navigating the highly nuanced waters of sexuality, orientation, and other LGBTQ-related conversations.

Dr. Steve Norman is a gifted speaker who has spent the last twenty-five years serving as a church planter, teaching pastor, and lead pastor. Steve uses humor, storytelling, practical illustrations, and his own personal experiences to communicate his messages. He holds a doctorate of missiology from Fuller Seminary and is passionate about helping individuals, families, churches, and businesses take the next step in their growth and development.

Dr. Peter Newhouse is the CEO of Winning At Home and oversees the Winning At Home Counseling Centers. He has been serving in the counseling field for more than twenty-five years and offers sound principles for everyday living that guide people toward healing outcomes. As an expert in the field of human relations, he enjoys providing practical solutions for communication and conflict management, depression, anxiety, anger management, pastoral and missionary care, post-traumatic stress disorder, premarital and marriage counseling, and a variety of other relationship topics. He seeks to help people know themselves and embrace who God designed them to be.

RECOMMENDED RESOURCES

Sex and Physical Development

How and When to Tell Your Kids about Sex: A Lifelong Approach to Shaping Your Child's Sexual Character
Stan and Brenna Jones

Before I Was Born: God Knew My Name
Carolyn Nystrom

The Story of Me: Babies, Bodies, and a Very Good God
Stan and Brenna Jones

What's the Big Deal?: Why God Cares about Sex
Stan and Brenna Jones

Facing the Facts: The Truth about Sex and You
Stan and Brenna Jones

Understanding Sexual Identity: A Resource for Youth Ministry
Mark Yarhouse

People to Be Loved: Why Homosexuality Is Not Just an Issue
Preston Sprinkle

Embodied: Transgender Identities, the Church, and What the Bible Has to Say
Preston Sprinkle

Journey Well: Explore Your Deepest Needs & How to Meet Them
Laurie Krieg with Matt Krieg

Our Bodies Tell God's Story: Discovering the Divine Plan for Love, Sex, and Gender
Christopher West

The Center for Faith, Sexuality & Gender: www.centerforfaith.com

General Parenting

The Secrets of Happy Families: Improve Your Mornings, Tell Your Family History, Fight Smarter, Go Out and Play, and Much More
Bruce Feiler

Parenting with Love and Logic: Teaching Children Responsibility
Foster Cline and Jim Fay

Shepherding a Child's Heart
Tedd Tripp

Parenting with Grace and Truth: Leading and Loving Your Kids Like Jesus
Dan Seaborn

Nurturing Great Kids Devotional
Dan Seaborn

Parenting Teens with Love and Logic: Preparing Adolescents for Responsible Adulthood
Jim Fay and Foster Cline

Growing With: Every Parent's Guide to Helping Teenagers and Young Adults Thrive in Their Faith, Family, and Future
Kara Powell and Steven Argue

Grace-Based Parenting: Set Your Family Free
Tim Kimmell

How to Really Love Your Child
Ross Campbell

Boundaries with Kids: How Healthy Choices Grow Healthy Children
Henry Cloud and John Townsend

Faith for Exiles: 5 Ways for a New Generation to Follow Jesus in Digital Babylon
David Kinnaman and Mark Matlock

The Intentional Father: A Practical Guide to Raise Sons of Courage and Character
Jon Tyson

Parenting: 14 Gospel Principles That Can Radically Change Your Family
Paul David Tripp

Brainstorm: The Power and Purpose of the Teenage Brain
Daniel Siegel

The Whole-Brain Child: 12 Revolutionary Strategies to Nurture Your Child's Developing Mind
Daniel Siegel and Tina Payne Bryson

Raising a Secure Child: How Circle of Security Parenting Can Help You Nurture Your Child's Attachment, Emotional Resilience, and Freedom to Explore
Kent Hoffman, Glen Cooper, Bert Powell, and Christine Benton

Untangled: Guiding Teenage Girls Through the Seven Transitions into Adulthood
Lisa Damour

Quiet: The Power of Introverts in a World That Can't Stop Talking
Susan Cain

The Connected Child: Bring Hope and Healing to Your Adoptive Family
Karyn B. Purvis, David R. Cross, and Wendy Lyons Sunshine

Communication

3 Big Questions That Change Every Teenager: Making the Most of Your Conversations and Connections
Kara Powell and Brad M. Griffin

How to Talk So Kids Will Listen and Listen So Kids Will Talk
Adele Faber and Elaine Mazlish

Mental Health

Anxiety Relief for Kids: On-the-Spot Strategies to Help Your Child Overcome Worry, Panic, and Avoidance
Bridget Flynn Walker

Why Am I Feeling Like This?: A Teen's Guide to Freedom from Anxiety and Depression
David Murray

Why Is My Teenager Feeling Like This?: A Guide for Helping Teens through Anxiety and Depression
David Murray

Parenting from the Inside Out: How a Deeper Self-Understanding Can Help You Raise Children Who Thrive
Dan Siegel

Raising Worry-Free Girls: Helping Your Daughter Feel Braver, Stronger, and Smarter in an Anxious World
Sissy Goff

Brave: A Teen Girl's Guide to Beating Worry and Anxiety
Sissy Goff

Braver, Stronger, Smarter: A Girl's Guide to Overcoming Worry & Anxiety
Sissy Goff

Under Pressure: Confronting the Epidemic of Stress and Anxiety in Girls
Lisa Damour

Technology

The Tech-Wise Family: Everyday Steps for Putting
Technology in Its Proper Place
Andy Crouch

Common Sense Media: www.commonsensemedia.org